THE
REAGAN
WIT

THE
REAGAN
WIT

Edited by
Bill Adler
with
Bill Adler, Jr.

CAROLINE HOUSE PUBLISHERS, INC.
Aurora, Illinois

10 9 8 7 6 5 4 3 2 1

Copies of this book may be purchased from the publisher for $6.95. All inquiries and catalog requests should be addressed to Caroline House Publishers, Inc., 920 West Industrial Drive, Aurora, IL 60506. (312) 897-2050.

ISBN: 0-89803-090-0
Designed by Irene Friedman

Library of Congress Cataloging in Publication Data

Reagan, Ronald.
  The Reagan wit.

  1. Reagan, Ronald—Quotations. I. Adler,
Bill. II. Adler, Bill, 1956-
III. Title.
E838.5.R435   1981   973.927′092′4   81-38509
ISBN 0-89803-090-0   AACR2

CONTENTS

INTRODUCTION

No one can face the awesome responsibilities of the presidency without a keen sense of wit and humor. Ronald Wilson Reagan, the fortieth President of the United States, perhaps more so than any of his predecessors displays an innate and superb wit. Ronald Reagan's unique sense of humor not only has helped him capture theatrical and political audiences, but has also been instrumental in his evolution from citizen to President. From his early days as a college student some fifty years ago, through his career as an actor, then governor of the most populous state in the Union, and finally President of the United States, Reagan's wit has supported him during many difficult times and helped to shape his remarkable career.

Reagan knows how to use his wit, how to defend himself with it, how to mold it into a formidable political weapon, how to poke fun at himself, and how to use it to defend ideas he believes are vital to the nation and world. But although he is cognizant of the usefulness of this important ability, Ronald Reagan's wit flows naturally and freely. It is a part of him and his personality.

The Reagan Wit offers anecdotes, humorous stories, and quips that span nearly the entire life of Ronald Reagan. It presents a penetrating and fascinating insight into the man, his personality, and beliefs. Through his wit we think that a new portrait of Ronald Wilson Reagan emerges.

Bill Adler
Bill Adler, Jr.
New York City
May 1981

1.
THE
ASSASSINATION
ATTEMPT

It may have saved his life. But at the very least, Ronald Reagan's wit and humor helped see the nation and the President through those dangerous and uncertain days. The President's sense of humor demonstrated clearly not only how important Reagan's wit is to himself, but also how vital it is to the entire nation. As the assassination attempt and aftermath revealed, Reagan's wit is more than just his ability to tell a good joke. His wit is in a class by itself; it acts as his sword and shield.

One of the doctors who treated the President said that Reagan's humor "made him more natural and easier to approach as a patient." And, indeed, his wit relaxed all Americans. The moment we heard reports about his humor in George Washington University Hospital, we knew he was all right.

I knew from the manner in which I was unclothed that I probably wouldn't wear that suit again.

Washington, D.C.
April 22, 1981

Soon after Reagan awoke, presidential aide Lyn Nofziger reported to Reagan, "You'll be happy to know that the government is running normally." The President replied without hesitation:

What makes you think I'd be happy about that?

Washington, D.C.
April 2, 1981

9

Note to doctors:

Send me to L.A., where I can see the air I'm breathing.
Washington, D.C.
March 31, 1981

To aide Deaver, Reagan remarked,

I really screwed up the schedule.
Washington, D.C.

When the President's California allergist, Dr. Ralph Book-man, stopped by Reagan's hospital room, the President told him,

Doc, you should have tested me for lead!
Washington, D.C.
April 12, 1981

I found out it hurts to get shot.
Washington, D.C.
April 12, 1981

Reflecting on the shooting, Reagan said,

I guess it goes with the territory.
Washington, D.C.
March 31, 1981

To the doctor who told the President that he's a good patient, Reagan replied,

I have to be. My father-in-law is a doctor.
Washington, D.C.
April 12, 1981

10

To his aides assembled at his hospital bedside:

Hi, fellas. I knew it would be too much to hope that we could skip a staff meeting.

Washington, D.C.
April 12, 1981

In a note to one of his early morning nurses, Reagan wrote,

If I knew I had such talent for this, I'd have tried it sooner.

Washington, D.C.
April 12, 1981

While in the hospital, Reagan used the excuse of having to use the toilet to give himself a cool sponge bath. Although he fooled the hospital staff, Reagan was worried about being discovered:

I thought they'd find out because I'd made such a mess, so I got down on my hands and knees and mopped up the floor so the nurse wouldn't find out.

Washington, D.C.
April 11, 1981

After waking from surgery, Reagan scribbled,

I'm still alive, aren't I?

Washington, D.C.
March 30, 1981

The President was more than curious about the man accused of shooting him:

Does anybody know what that guy's beef was?

Washington, D.C.
March 31, 1981

11

The President was overjoyed to learn that Secret Service agent Timothy J. McCarthy, Officer Thomas K. Delahanty of the District of Columbia Police, and White House Press Secretary Jim Brady were improving after being shot:

That's great news, just great, especially about Jim. We'll have to get four bedpans and have a reunion.

Washington, D.C.
April 4, 1981

To wife Nancy the President offered a simple apology:

Honey, I forgot to duck.

Washington, D.C.
March 30, 1981

Not realizing that he had been shot, President Reagan first thought that the Secret Service agent's efforts to get him into the limousine were too forceful.

I've got to apologize to that guy. I accused him of breaking my ribs.

Washington, D.C.
March 31, 1981

If I'd gotten this much attention in Hollywood, I never would have left.

Washington, D.C.
March 30, 1981

To a nurse at George Washington Hospital who told the President, ''Keep up the good work,'' Reagan replied,

You mean this may happen several times more?

Washington, D.C.
March 31, 1981

The President wanted to make sure that his surgeons were qualified:

I hope you're all Republicans.

Washington, D.C.
March 30, 1981

Reagan's first public appearance after the assassination attempt was before a joint session of Congress. He received a tumultuous standing ovation.

Thank you. You wouldn't want to talk me into an encore?

Washington, D.C.
April 28, 1980

To his daughter, Maureen, President Reagan pointed out another misfortune of the attempt:

Ruined one of my best suits.

Washington, D.C.
March 30, 1981

After entering the hospital, the President queried an attractive nurse,

Does Nancy know about us?

Washington, D.C.
April 1, 1981

I always heal fast.

Washington, D.C.
March 31, 1981

In a note to the doctors, Reagan quoted Winston Churchill:

13

There is no more exhilarating feeling than being shot without result.

Washington, D.C.
March 31, 1981

In his speech before Congress, Reagan said,

The society we heard from is made up of millions of compassionate Americans and their children, from college age to kindergarten.

As a matter of fact, as evidence of that I have a letter with me. The letter came from Peter Sweeney. He's in the second grade in the Riverdale School in Rockville Center. And he said: "I hope you get well quick for you might have to make a speech in your pajamas."

And he added a postscript: "P.S. If you have to make a speech in your pajamas, I warned you."

Washington, D.C.
April 28, 1981

Reagan reported to the American people,

Thanks to some very fine people, my health is much improved. I'd like to be able to say that with regard to the health of the economy.

Washington, D.C.
April 28, 1981

At one point the President scribbled a paraphrase of W. C. Fields,

All in all, I'd rather be in Philadelphia.

Washington, D.C.
March 30, 1981

14

I don't think I'm going to hurdle any tables in the room here for a while.

Washington, D.C.
April 22, 1981

The day after the assassination attempt, Reagan quipped,

Don't worry. I'll get out of this.

Washington, D.C.
March 31, 1981

To the newly elected White House Press Association president, Clifford Evans, Reagan said,

As one President to another, let me give you some advice. When someone tells you to get into the car, do it—quickly.

Washington, D.C.
April 26, 1981

Reporter: What are you going to do first when you get home, Mr. President?

Reagan: Sit down.

Washington, D.C.
April 11, 1981

The President displayed his concern about the others who had been shot:

I didn't want a supporting cast.

Washington, D.C.
March 31, 1981

2.
THE
EARLY
YEARS

It was not long after he entered Eureka College that Ronald Reagan's unique wit and sense of humor emerged. Considered a very likable person by everyone who came into contact with him, he was also known to be a genuinely funny individual. His wit provided an escape valve for him during difficult moments in college, and proved invaluable in propelling the young Reagan first into a brief career as a radio sportscaster and then into a career as a successful movie star. Ronald Reagan looks back on these days with a good deal of humor, because much of what happened to him was indeed amusing.

It was during his years as an actor and later president of the Screen Actor's Guild that Reagan became involved in the fight against communism. His humor presents excellent insight into the formation of Reagan's newfound political direction. Reagan's wit shows the evolution of many conceptions that have come to play an important part in his role as President.

But above all, it was in his early years that we see the beginnings of the delightful Reagan wit.

Our family didn't exactly come from the wrong side of the tracks, but we were certainly always within the sound of the train whistles.

Recalling his early days as a lifeguard, Reagan wrote,

The only money I ever got was ten dollars for diving for an old man's upper plate that he lost going down our slide.

Reagan writes about his years as a football player:

I never thought seriously about retiring from the junior mayhem, but I managed to time my charge so that I was in one of the upper layers of bodies. The lure of sweat and action always pulled me back to the game—despite the fact that I was a scrawny, undersized, underweight nuisance, who insisted on getting in the way of the more skillful (such as my brother). As a result, I had a collection of the largest purplish-black bruises possible. More than once, I must have been a walking coagulation. Those were the happiest times of my life.

As a young man, Reagan once parked his Model T Ford near a lamp post, which he climbed. Soon after, a police officer drove up to the young Reagan and asked him what he was doing up there. Reagan replied,

Twinkle, twinkle, little star, just who do you think you are?

Reagan was fined a dollar.

Reagan was once stricken with viral pneumonia so badly that he recalls he almost decided to stop breathing, but a nurse persuaded him to take another breath and

she was *so* nice and persistent that I let her have her way.

About his first trip to Chicago, Reagan said:

I couldn't afford cabs and I was afraid of the damn buses—as a matter of fact, the city itself scared the bejesus out of me. Everybody seemed to know where they were going and what they were doing, and I could get lost just looking for a men's room.

As a sports broadcaster, young Reagan occasionally encountered unique challenges:

The Cubs and the St. Louis Cards were locked in a scoreless tie: Dizzy Dean on the mound, Billy Jurges at bat for the Cubs in the ninth inning. I saw Curly start to type so I finished the wind-up and had Dean send the ball on its way to the plate, took the slip from Curly, and found myself faced with the terse note: "The wire's gone dead." I had a ball on the way to the plate and there was no way to call it back. At the same time, I was convinced that a ball game tied up in the ninth inning was no time to tell my audience we had lost contact with the game and they would have to listen to recorded music. I knew of only one thing that wouldn't get in the score column and betray me—a foul ball. So I had Billy foul this pitch down the left field line. I looked expectantly at Curly. He just shrugged helplessly, so I had Billy foul another one, and still another; then he fouled one back into the box seats.

I described in detail the redheaded kid who had scrambled and gotten the souvenir ball. He fouled one into the upper deck that just missed being a home run. He fouled for six minutes and forty-five seconds until I lost count. I began to be frightened that maybe I was establishing a new world record for a fellow staying at bat hitting fouls, and this could betray me. Yet I was into it so far I didn't dare reveal that the wire had gone dead.

My voice was rising in pitch and threatening to crack—and then, bless him, Curly started typing. I clutched at the slip. It said: "Billy popped out on the first ball pitched." Not in my game he didn't—he popped out after practically making a career of foul balls.

About his years at college, Reagan wites:

There was the big gala watermelon hunt. We herded a few carefully indoctrinated freshmen out into the country by night and indicated a plot where we could swipe some of the bulging fruit from the vine. Tiptoeing through the patch to build up suspense, and at a prearranged location, the place exploded with light. A shotgun blast went off. An upper classman near me collapsed with a scream, gripping his chest, red fluid flowing slowly between his fingers. "I'm shot," he screamed. "My God, I am shot!" To add to his overacting, a flashlight gave a quick look at his catsup-covered midsection. A well-trained supporting cast, using some version of subliminal selling, shoved the freshmen toward the road, screaming, "Get help—a doctor—run back to town!" Other things were said, but these were the key words, repeated often enough to stick.

The frosh took off like leaves before the wind, propelled by fear and charity. We ran a few steps, then let them get ahead and watched them disappear. We hiked back to town by another and shorter road.

This particular night the freshmen ran nearly eight miles, probably setting some unofficial records (we never bothered to time them). But one fellow had retained his wits long enough to duck into a farmhouse on the main road halfway back to the college. He had wakened the old boy and they phoned a doctor in town, giving the location of the shooting and all the lurid details. Through the night, on his errand of mercy, sped the doctor. The slower return trip gave him time to do a little two-plus-two comes-up-college type of figuring. At the end of that month, each fraternity on the campus received a bill. It read: "For battle, murder, and sudden death at the watermelon patch—$10." Each fraternity paid without protest.

As an actor, Reagan once received an urgent telegram from his agent, Bill Meilkjohn: WARNER'S OFFER CONTRACT SEVEN YEARS, ONE YEAR'S OPTIONS, STARTING AT $200 A WEEK. WHAT SHALL I DO?

Reagan shot back his reply:

SIGN BEFORE THEY CHANGE THEIR MINDS.

A lot of the crying sounds coming out of our studios today are like a guy sitting on a nail, too lazy to get up from what's hurting him.

1956

Reagan recalls the challenge he faced from the Dead End Kids:

I did a string of pictures with the Dead End Kids, which was an experience similar to going over Niagara Falls in a barrel the hard way—upstream. Counting noises and getting them all in one scene was a major chore, but sometimes it was a relief when they did take off and disappear for a few hours. You never knew when a canvas chair would go up in smoke, or be blown apart by the giant firecrackers they were never without. Having heard lurid tales from other actors, I approached my first picture with them in something of a sweat. Jimmy Cagney solved my problem one noon at the corner table. Having had his beginnings in the same New York Hell's Kitchen, he understood these kids as no one else could. "It's very simple," he said. "Just tell them you look forward to working with them but you'll slap hell out of them if they do one thing out of line." He was right—it was just that simple. I had the only unscorched chair on the set.

Reagan writes about one of his movies:

One big action scene involved a gang fight with goons smashing up a truckload of crated tomatoes. For three nights we wallowed around in those tomatoes—the same tomatoes. By the third night the prop men were scooping them up with shovels and slopping them back into the crates for the next shot. At midnight we called a halt for lunch, our clothes plastered with wet squashed tomatoes, so that no one felt like putting on a coat or sweater over the mess in spite of the cold night air. Suddenly there was a roar of anger from

21

the first men in line, who happened to be stuntmen. The next thing we knew, a frightened caterer was sprinting out into the darkness across the tomato field with six burly stuntmen after him. The damn fool was serving stewed tomatoes.

About one incident during his army tour, Reagan writes:

At an advance air base in France, Norman Krasna found a lonely cross on the far side of the airstrip. There was no name, no epitaph, just the date: December 24, 1944. All of his playwright's instinct was aroused by this lonely cross, which evidently marked the final resting place of an unknown soldier who had died on Christmas Eve.

He knew that somehow it must be worked into the finished film. He photographed the cross against the blue sky, then waited hours to get it starkly silhouetted against the sunset. He even crept over to photograph it in the swirling mists of early dawn. He had hundreds of feet of color film, taken at every hour of the day and from every conceivable angle. Finally he needed more than film, so he revealed his secret in the officer's mess and demanded to know if there wasn't someone present who knew the history of this unnamed grave. He was met with blank surprise: no one had knowledge of any grave. They asked him just where this thing was located. He could tell them its exact whereabouts—he had practically worn a path across the airstrip leading to it. Suddenly, light dawned. The army dates and marks buried latrines in this manner, so they won't be reopened before nature and quicklime have done their disease-preventive work. Norman possessed the most color footage of a latrine in army history.

Referring to his army career, Reagan quipped:

Colonel Ferguson turned me over to the adjutant at Fort Mason on the first day of my military service. I discovered

that, even though I was in, another physical was required. I went through the same old business with the eyes, and one of the two examining doctors said, "If we sent you overseas, you'd shoot a general."

The other doctor looked up and said, "Yes, and you'd miss him."

Ronald Reagan on acting:

Today, however, if I could give one bit of advice to youngsters starting out in theater or movies I'd say: Don't marry your leading lady or leading man until you've done another role opposite someone else. Leadingladyitis is an infatuation that won't hold up, once the play is over and you each go back to playing yourselves.

Reagan appeared in many movies during his acting career. Regarding those films, he writes:

The studio didn't want good—it wanted them Thursday.

In one movie scene, actor Ronald Reagan was shot in the chest. After the assailant departed, Reagan removed from his front shirt pocket a dictionary with a bullet embedded in it, and kissed the book. He then put it in his hip pocket,

in the event that the next time he might shoot me in the fanny.

At three o'clock in the morning we were shooting a scene around a campfire where, as cavalry officers, we were listening with amusement to the prophecies of an old Indian woman. Errol [Flynn] moved over to the director, had a whispered consultation, and a moment later my position in the group was changed, putting me behind a couple of other actors who had lesser roles but more height.

During the rehearsal I realized that I wouldn't even be visible to the camera above the shoulders of the men in front of me. I figured that under the rules of the game I was entitled to protect myself, so as the rehearsal went on I kept quietly scraping a pile of loose earth together with my feet. I didn't make use of it in the rehearsal, but when the cameras rolled, I quietly stepped up on my newly created gopher mound. When the time came for my one line in the scene it dropped like the gentle rain from heaven on the heads of the men in front.

Reagan discussed a film of his:

I saw *Knute Rockne* one night, and it was so hacked up, my eighty-yard run was a five-yard loss.

During a fight scene while filming a movie, Reagan accidentally knocked down a stuntman. He recalls:

Enter Stuntman Number Two. In the course of routining our fight, I told him of what had happened and said, ''I sure hope I never do that again.'' Quietly he informed me he knew it had happened; the downed stuntman was his roommate.

On the third day of our fight there was another accident—only this time I had one eye closed, with a beautiful purple mouse. He was properly apologetic—strangely enough, in almost the same words I had used to his roommate.

Ronald Reagan was courting the former Nancy Davis. While attending a Motion Picture Industry Council meeting one night with fellow actor Bill Holden, Reagan scribbled a note to him:

To hell with this, how would you like to be best man when I marry Nancy?

Holden replied out loud: "It's about time."

While on the subject of conservation—a subject that has been dear to me for many years and on which I have spoken and written from the heart many times—I feel impelled, at this time, to express my animosity toward what I call "plinkers." In referring to "plinkers" I do not by any means mean the serious hunter in search of game; I mean those people who, with gun in hand, and no serious purpose in mind, get an itch to pull a trigger and "plink," there goes a robin or an oriole. Just because they wondered: "Could I?"

1965

On defending our political system against communism, Reagan once told an audience that the need to fight is immediate:

If they were so complacent as to think they could sit back and not lift a hand until the battle involved them personally, they were about as shortsighted as a fellow going into the poultry business without a rooster—they were putting a hell of a lot of confidence in the stork.

Recalling his days as a "hemophilic liberal," Reagan wrote in his autobiography:

I have come to realize that a great many so-called liberals aren't liberal—they will defend to the death your right to agree with them.

1966

3.
THE
CAMPAIGN
FOR
GOVERNOR

Some analysts maintain that it was Reagan's unique political abilities and Governor Pat Brown's waning public support that enabled Ronald Reagan to capture the governorship in 1966. Although it is true that the Reagan campaign displayed superior tactics and that Reagan himself was able to make excellent use of the media, his wit, used casually and often, was an essential tool in his campaign for governorship.

Reagan was able to employ his sense of humor and wit in his first political contest much as a fine fencer wields a saber. His jabs were direct, but he knew when to retreat and turn his wit around to defend his position on an issue. During the campaign for governor of California, the public was introduced to the delightful Reagan wit.

Suddenly now that I want to be something else besides an actor, everybody is saying that I'm an actor. I'll probably be the only fellow who will get an Oscar posthumously.
Orange County, Calif.
March 30, 1966

Reagan responded to many of the letters he received:

Mrs. Smith Ely Jelliffe
19 Alden Place
Bronxville, New York

Dear Mrs. Jelliffe:

Thanks very much for your letter. Unfortunately it didn't arrive in time to save me. I am now a candidate

29

for governor.

Let's just put it this way. We'll give the Republicans one more chance to see whether they'd rather fight than vote. If they don't reform, I'll join you in your retirement from politics and you can teach me the pleasures of wondering.

Best regards,

Ronald Reagan

January 13, 1966

Reagan commented during a drive past Disneyland:

In my position, you know, you can't just wander around. You are a tourist attraction yourself.

1965

Government is like a baby—an alimentary canal with a big appetite at one end and no sense of responsibility at the other.

1965

Keeping up with Governor Brown's promises is like reading *Playboy* magazine while your wife turns the pages.

1966

Reagan on an actor becoming governor of California:

I don't know—I've never played a governor before.

August 3, 1965

When asked, during his first campaign for governor, what his main campaign issue was, Reagan quipped,

To retire Pat Brown.

1966

Reagan was not very sensitive to the charge that he had no political experience:

I don't know of anybody who was born holding public office. I am not a professional politician. The man who currently has the job has more political experience than anybody. That's why I'm running.

1966

We are told that God is dead. Well, He isn't. We just can't talk to Him in the classroom anymore.

Commenting on Governor Pat Brown:

The governor talks about *his* dams and *his* lakes and *his* reservoirs; you have the feeling that when he leaves office he'll take them with him.

And again:

Well, he's good to his family . . . he's put a lot of relatives on the payroll.

1966

I have an opponent who says money is the mother's milk of politics, and you've never seen a baby who has so much squawk about where the milk comes from.

1969

Candidate Reagan took issue with pornography in California:

The biggest joke in Paris, France, is that instead of selling French postcards, they're selling California postcards.

1966

31

Speaking in the vegetable-growing region of California to a group of women, Ronald Reagan pointed out his concern for the high cost of living:

You ladies know that if you stand in front of the asparagus counter at the supermarket these days, it's cheaper to eat money.

Reagan occasionally joked about the charge that he received support from the John Birch Society and other ultraconservative groups, and often would begin his speeches by saying:

Gentlemen—and little ladies in tennis shoes.

1966

Once upon a time, the only contact with government was when you went to buy a stamp.

1965

Although many assumed that Reagan would soon issue a formal declaration of his candidacy, the then noncandidate said,

I've also said, of course, you keep one foot back in case the sky starts to fall.

1966

President Dewey warned me not to get overconfident.

1966

Politics is just like show business. You need a big opening. Then you coast for a while. Then you need a big finish.

1966

Referring to liberals, Reagan commented,

The labels somehow got pasted on the wrong people.

4.
THE
YEARS
AS
GOVERNOR

To go from a career as a movie actor to governor of the largest, most diverse state in the nation requires a great deal of courage. It also requires a sense of humor.

There is no doubt that his keen wit immensely aided Reagan in dealing with the endless problems and numerous individuals he encountered as governor. His eight-year term coincided with the turbulent late sixties and early seventies, a time when the nation and California were torn by an undeclared war, campus unrest, open experimentation with drugs and sex, and a general feeling of lack of national direction. Reagan's wit and humor not only assisted in his fight to protect his administration and state from disorder, but also helped win the hearts of the people of California.

At his midnight gubernatorial inauguration, Reagan remarked to George Murphy, dancer-turned-senator:

George, here we are on the late show again.

January 3, 1967

Soon after he was elected governor, Reagan's campaign staff left. Reagan said to his then press secretary, Lyn Nofziger,

My God, what do we do now?

1967

I wasn't quite prepared for a schedule that's more strict and busier than a baby's formula.

1967

Soon after assuming the governorship, Reagan was faced with a hostile press. He remarked,

If this has been a honeymoon, then I've been sleeping alone.

1967

Reporter: The Gallup poll shows that your popularity as a potential presidential candidate is slipping. How do you explain that?

Reagan: I regard that as a tribute to my efforts to convince people I'm not a candidate.

1967

When asked by a hostile reporter about the qualifications of his appointees, Reagan gibed,

If I appointed him, he's qualified.

1967

When on Lincoln's birthday the entire gubernatorial staff showed up for work, while most other state employees did not, Reagan quipped,

I just invited them to the party. They didn't *have* to come.

1967

Speech by Gov. Ronald Reagan to the National Sheriff's Association:

It's a pleasure to be here today—where the heat only comes from the sun.

Las Vegas is really a wonderful place. Where else outside of government do people throw money away. The big difference, of course, is that here you can do it yourself; in government, we do it for you.

But it's nice to see all you sheriffs out there. I've been

36

a sheriff myself—you can't make a living in Hollywood for more than twenty-five years without being a sheriff, and if the picture makes money, polish the star, you'll wear it often.

Las Vegas, Nev.
June 19, 1967

A computer error brought Reagan's Democratic predecessor, Edmund G. Brown, a Republican fundraising letter signed by Gov. Ronald Reagan. The following correspondence resulted:

Dear Hon. Reagan:

In today's mail I received a letter from you recalling the days of the Brown-Unruh clique.

I am very interested in your record of increased taxation, increased welfare costs and property taxes.

I really believe that Edmund G. Brown, Jr., will do a far better job than your hand-picked candidate, Houston Flournoy. I must, therefore, refuse your kind invitation to contribute to the Republican State Central Committee.

Sincerely,

Edmund G. Brown

Dear Pat:

I just thought that you might be ready to do penance.

Sincerely,

Ronald W. Reagan

37

I've never been able to understand how the Democrats can run those $1,000-a-plate dinners at such a profit, and run the government at such a loss.

Dallas, Tex.
October 26, 1967

At Republican fundraising dinner:

Two and a half years ago we put a new captain (President Nixon) on the barnacle-encrusted ship of state. And now, the people who allowed that ship to become encrusted and swerve off course blame the captain for not providing an instant moonlight cruise.

Framingham, Mass.
June 14, 1971

One way to make sure crime doesn't pay would be to let the government run it.

Dallas, Tex.
October 26, 1967

When asked about Nelson Rockefeller's presidential aspirations, Reagan said,

You're asking the wrong noncandidate. Ask him.

1967

As photographers continued to click away at the governor, they kept asking him to smile. Reagan responded:

If I keep on smiling, it looks like I have a very light-hearted speech.

Photographer: Will you gesture, Governor?

Reagan: I don't gesture very much when I talk.

The cameras keep snapping away, and finally Reagan said:

Now, you *will* get all these published?

1967

Responding to a young man's comment that former actor, now Governor Ronald Reagan makes a good good guy, "and a better bad guy," he said,

Of course. You know it takes more acting to be a bad guy.

1967

Looking back at his first few months as governor, Reagan joked,

There was a time back around January when I felt like an Egyptian tank driver with a set of Russian instructions.

1967

When those who are governed do too little, those who govern can—and often will—do too much.

Inauguration address
Sacramento, Calif.
January 4, 1971

When speculation increased about Reagan's becoming a candidate for the Republican nomination for President, a reporter asked if he would issue a Sherman statement. Reagan replied,

I never found anyone but Sherman who ever said that, so I figure it's his line.

1968

Commenting on his newly acquired estate, Reagan observed,

I'm not one to look a gift house in the mouth.

Sacramento, Calif.
February 3, 1967

Reagan's response to the reporter who asked if the governor would run for Vice President if asked was quick:

Before or after I fainted?

When he returned to his home state of Illinois, Reagan said,

It is a homecoming for me and I could be very nostalgic. Of course when I lived here before, I was a Democrat and my whole family were Democrats. As a matter of fact, I had an uncle who lived here in Chicago who won a medal once for never having missed voting in an election for fifteen years . . . and he had been dead for fourteen.

August 9, 1973

Do you remember back in the days when you thought that nothing could replace the dollar. Today it practically has!

August 9, 1973

Fleas are a part of the ecological cycle, but I doubt if a dog thinks he is doing something to destroy ecology by wearing a flea collar.

March 7, 1973

Heaven help us if government ever gets into the business of protecting us from ourselves.

April 12, 1973

40

There are some days you go home so frustrated that you get in the shower and you make speeches to the walls of the shower. But there are other days when you go home and feel ten feet tall because you have solved a problem.

March 8, 1973

When I was first governor it seemed like every day brought more and more problems, but one day I was on the way to the office when I heard a disc jockey who became a great favorite of mine. Out of the clear blue sky he said, "Everybody should take unto himself a wife, because sooner or later something is bound to happen you can't blame on the governor."

August 9, 1973

I have learned that one of the most important rules in politics is poise—which means looking like an owl after you have behaved like a jackass.

August 9, 1973

They [those responsible for Watergate] did something that was stupid and foolish and was criminal—it was illegal. Illegal is a better word than criminal, because I think criminal has a different connotation. I think the tragedy of this is that men who are not criminals at heart, and certainly not engaged in criminal activities, committed a criminal or illegal act and now must bear the consequences. These are men whose lives are being very much changed by this. I doubt if any of them would even intentionally double-park.

Sacramento, Calif.
May 1, 1973

There is no shortage of energy with which we run the government of California, which we run on jellybeans!

April 26, 1974

[Carving a turkey] was something I had to learn after I grew up, because when I was a kid we couldn't afford a turkey.

November 14, 1973

When asked by a reporter to recall the nicest thing a girl ever did for him, the governor wrote:

The nicest thing a girl ever did for me was when a girl named Nancy married me and brought a warmth and joy to my life that has grown with each passing year.

I know she won't mind if I say the second nicest thing was a letter from a little fifth grade girl last week. She added a P.S., "You devil, you." I've walked with a swagger ever since.

1971

While attending a board of regents meeting in California, university officials were discussing how the proposed Reagan cuts would harm the university. The governor drew a cartoon of Chicken Little carrying a mortarboard on her head crying,

The sky is falling! The sky is falling!

1967

Speaking to a group of middle-aged labor leaders:

You youngsters probably don't remember, but when I was young, golf was a sissy, rich man's game. So were boating and skiing and horseback riding. Today they're weekend sports for the working man; he doesn't have to go to Labor Day picnics.

Labor Day 1970

I'm just a citizen temporarily in public service.

1970

Reagan once said that his "feet [were] in concrete" against a state withholding tax system. When he reversed his position, the governor told reporters,

Gentlemen, that noise you hear is the concrete breaking up around my feet.

1970

Speech to the California State Bar Association:

Why does a criminal defendant with a clever lawyer seem able to run circles around some of our finest prosecutors with a seemingly bottomless barrel of time-consumer tricks? The public is frustrated and fed up with the sort of behavior that some defendants—and, indeed, some of their lawyers—are seemingly able to get away with in courtrooms, behavior that would not be tolerated in any kindergarten.

Los Angeles, Calif.
September 20, 1970

I sometimes think if someone applied the Ten Commandments to some of our courts, they would rule—"Thou shalt not, unless you feel strongly to the contrary."

June 22, 1973

43

Bobby Kennedy is making Lyndon Johnson so nervous he's thinking of putting the country in his wife's name.

Dallas, Tex.
October 26, 1967

The crime problem has indeed become a matter of wide-spread concern, even among people of different philosophies. Today's hardliner on law and order is yesterday's liberal who was mugged last night.

August 1, 1973

When asked by a reporter what he would have done in response to North Korea's seizure of the USS Pueblo, *Governor Reagan replied,*

I don't command any ships. California doesn't have a navy.

Jesse Unruh was the opposition leader in the California legislature while Reagan was governor. In a letter to Lt. Gov. Robert Finch, who was going to take charge of the state during the governor's absence, Reagan added a P.S.:

Bob, I'd like you to have the cornerstone of the new mansion laid by my return. Preferably with Jesse Unruh in it.

Reagan remarked to his secretary, Kathy Davis,

I have two favorite records for this music box. This one is "Silent Night." It's good for the office Christmas party. [The other one is] Mendelssohn's "Wedding March." Hmmnn, I wonder if I have the power to marry people. Could you get a legal ruling on that, Kathy?

44

If we gave the vote to eighteen-year-olds, the next President of the United States will have three things to worry about: Vietnam, inflation, and acne.

At annual Host Breakfast
Sacramento, Calif.
September 4, 1970

In my country some twenty-five years ago, you could make a long-distance call on a privately owned telephone system from San Francisco to New York for $28. For that same amount of money, you could send 1,376 letters. Today, you can make the same telephone call for two dollars and a half and for that amount you can only send 41 letters. So the government is investigating the Bell System!

London, England
February 2, 1970

To blame the military for war makes about as much sense as suggesting that we get rid of cancer by getting rid of doctors.

At University of California
at Los Angeles
June 7, 1970

Soon after inauguration day, the governor's landlord threatened to sell the house that a group of friends had joined together to purchase in order to rent it back to Ronald Reagan, since the governor's mansion was very rundown and a firetrap. The result was a "Dear Landlord" letter, a copy of which went to every member of the group:

Knowing you receive unjustified complaints and undeserved criticism from miserable and unhappy tenants, and having a peculiar sympathy for anyone subject to that kind of treatment, I thought you might enjoy hearing from a happy tenant for a change.

My wife and I are very glad you bought out our previous

landlord. (He should lose the money on the way to the bank.) Somehow, the place looks brighter already, possibly because we've painted a little here and there. (We won't knock out any walls, however, without letting you know.)

Anyway, the hot water is hot when it should be; the neighbors are quiet. (If they complain, they'll get a freeway right through their piazza.) The fuses don't blow, not even with all the lights on, and it's only ten minutes to my job.

Just changing landlords has my wife so revved up she is pushing furniture all over the place. (Frankly, it gives me a pain in the back.) But we want you to know we love you, we thank you heartily, and if keeping the place real nice will help show our appreciation, we'll do it. We don't even let the dog in the house, and the kids are severely limited. P.S.: I am talking to the people I work for about lowering your taxes.

1967

Briefed before drawing up his first state budget, Reagan quipped:

What I have recently learned about the state of finances in California, we may turn out to be the first state that ever ran on Diner's Club cards.

1967

Let me get on the bandwagon with a counterpoint to the young pot smoker's plea or plaint. In New York recently at a dinner party a prominent editor sought the advice of several of us on "What do you tell a teenager who uses pot?" I suspect he was really asking "What do I do about my son?" I volunteered a few logical approaches, all of which he rejected. Finally (a little short of temper) I said, "Why don't you tell him if you catch him with one of those things in his mouth you'll kick his bottom side up between his shoulders?" Of course, he rejected that too.

46

In response to a constituent's letter about women's liberation, the governor wrote:

I have read your letter anent ribs and women with great interest.

I am pleased to tell you I share your views about women's liberation. At the same time, I have to say I'm greatly pleased with the twenty-three ribs that have been assigned to me under the marital customs of our society. While I feel no need personally for the proposal you make to restore the equity in the matter of the missing rib, I have asked my legal advisers to look into all the ramifications of such a change in the law.

However, and above all, I want to thank you from the bottom of my heart for your letter. Your complaint about the missing rib is the only thing I haven't been blamed for since I've been in this damn job.

Their signs said make love, not war, but they didn't look like they could do either.

1969

There's an old legend about the politician who looks out his window and sees his constituents marching by. "There go my people," he says. "I must hasten to find out where they're going so I can get in front and lead them."

Reagan had a few thoughts for the antiwar protesters:

Those young people [demand] the right to send blood to the enemy in Vietnam. I think they should be allowed to do that—providing they send it in the original container.

Reagan questioned America's motivation in Vietnam:

Somehow we are unable or at least unwilling to bring

47

to terms, or force to an armistice, a ramshackle water-buffalo economy with a gross national budget hardly equal to that of Pascagoula, Mississippi.

In the final days of his administration, Gov. Pat Brown made eighty judicial appointments. About this Reagan lamented,

I'm probably the only governor who can't fix a parking ticket.

In response to some advice offered by Washington governor Daniel Evans on how to deal with college students, Reagan wrote:

Dear Dan,

Thanks so much for the brochure; I agree you have a right to be proud.

How would you feel about an exchange program with a choice selection from our Berkeley campus?

Best regards,

Ron

1967

When asked if he would approve a withholding tax bill in California, the governor replied:

[Only] if they held a hot iron to my feet and I was bound hand and foot.

1967

If a bureaucrat had been writing the Ten Commandments, a simple rock slab would not have been near enough room.

Those simple rules would have read: "Thou shalt not, unless you feel strongly to the contrary, or for the following stated exceptions, see paragraphs 1–10, subsection no. A."

June 6, 1974

If you want to know which way to go in the future, you have to know which path you took in the past and where you stepped in a gopher hole along the way.

October 15, 1974

When asked what impact the candidacy of Sen. Eugene McCarthy would have on President Johnson's prospects for reelection, Reagan said,

This is the type of McCarthyism I heartily approve of—anything that's divisive among Democrats is constructive to Republicans.

Yale University
New Haven, Conn.
1967

At first, Reagan had told reporters that there would be no budget cuts for the University of California. When he changed his mind, the governor told reporters,

I goofed.

News conference
January 17, 1968

Commenting on the exploitation of California's resources by other states, Governor Reagan said:

The symbol of our state flag is a golden bear. It is not a cow to be milked.

1967

Sometimes you might think they have a military wedding, you know, crossed welfare checks.

December 14, 1967

When asked by a reporter whether he would look with an open mind at a particular bill before the California legislature, Reagan said,

Oh, certainly! Heavens, contrary to what some people in the back of the room believe, I look at everything with an open mind before I vote no.

The polls say I am doing all right with the men but I am way, way down with the women. Now maybe I am missing something, and you gals can help me. They say the women like Ronnie Ree-gin's charm. Now if you girls can give me a few tips, it would really help.

You know California doesn't have a foreign policy.

1968

The governor's mansion was situated near a well-trafficked street. Reagan more than once complained about the noise to his secretary, Kathy Davis:

Kathy, those damn trucks! I think they shift gears every time I begin falling asleep.

Referring to the Democrats, Reagan said,

The difference between them and us, is that *we* want to check government spending, and *they* want to spend government checks.

50

Immediately after asking the California legislature for a record $946 million tax increase, Governor Reagan had to leave for New York. Noting his good fortune, Reagan commented,

Pretty good timing. I'll drop the tax message and run.

1967

I sometimes wonder what the Ten Commandments would have looked like if Moses had to run them through a Democratic legislature.

1969

The credibility gap is so great in Washington they told us the truth the other day hoping we wouldn't believe it.

1969

To a gathering of state Republicans Reagan commented on his troubles with the Democrats:

As you can well imagine, my mind has been turning back to that first time we met under these same circumstances four years ago. Then we were in the first month of a brand new administration. Now it is the first month of a second term and we are all a little older, a little wiser—and still a few votes short in the legislature.

There's something about football that no other game has. There's sort of a mystique about it. It's a game in which you can feel a clean hatred for your opponent.

December 19, 1971

I have an abiding love for the game. Maybe at this moment I should be drawing a parallel with someone else—a freshman at Notre Dame in the days of Knute Rockne. The squad was so big on opening day of football practice that

51

Rock decided to thin it out in a rather primitive manner. He lined them up in two lines facing each other and put a soccer ball down between them. Then he explained that they would loosen up by trying to kick the ball over each other's goal line. And he made it clear that in the process a few shins might get kicked but football called for courage so that should not stop them. Then he looked down and the ball had disappeared. He said, "All right, where is it—who took the soccer ball?" The pint-sized freshman said, "Never mind the ball, Rock—when do we start kicking?"

1971

The self-proclaimed revolutionaries and their legal champions denounce the "system" . . . yet they wrap themselves in the Constitution at every step in legal proceedings that involve them. To accept their idea of "justice" is to accept tyranny and anarchy. If Moses himself stood on Nob Hill [in San Francisco] and solemnly intoned the Ten Commandments, he probably would be denounced as a reactionary seeking to impose a repressive and outmoded lifestyle on the multitude.

December 2, 1971

To the reporter who wanted to know what Reagan had learned so far on the school finance problem, he said,

Not to answer your question.

1971

And to another reporter who wanted to know if Reagan thought he would stay out of the 1976 presidential contest if Sen. Edward Kennedy ran, Reagan retorted,

This is a great place to say "no comment."

As I told a group of your fellow citizens who visited the capitol last fall, if California's problems and California's people were put in a ring together, it would have to be declared a mismatch.

1971

Remembering our last meeting here under these same circumstances and in spite of the general belief that pain cannot be relived in memory, I recalled the cold of that day four years ago and decided that cold's ability to shrink and contract should be applied to my remarks. We will soon be indoors and thawed out!

I do not know whether time has a faster pace in Sacramento than elsewhere but these four years have gone by more swiftly than they did when I marked a four-year term as the period from freshman to senior. And yet in this four-year span we have plumbed the ocean depths and reached out to the stars. We have lived for extended periods on the ocean's floor and have walked on the surface of the moon. In fact, I have been up in the air a few times myself and once or twice have sought advice about living under water.

Inauguration speech
1971

Hysterical pollution leads to political pollution with the result that all too often little or nothing gets done about actual pollution.

A Sacramento schoolteacher wrote the governor:

I thought you might enjoy a little humor today which happened in my kindergarten class.

I was briefing my class on the field trip we were to take the following day. One of the places scheduled to visit was the governor's mansion.

53

"Does anyone know who is the governor of California?" I asked.

(Complete silence)

"Oh, come now, children, you know his name. Ronald ———?" (I hinted).

Instantly twenty-three hands shot up and twenty-three voices shouted triumphantly—

"RONALD MCDONALD!"

The governor replied:

I did get a kick out of it. I guess television has more power than any of us know.

I'll return the favor by telling you of the teacher who taught her class about magnets and their properties and then several weeks later gave a test and asked them what it was that was spelled with six letters, began with an *M*, and picked up things. Eighty-seven percent of the class said "mother." The true television anecdote, however, is the child who told her mother she liked her better than the other leading brands.

Thanks again, and please give my greetings to your class. Tell them I don't mind being Ronald McDonald at all.

When the governor learned that the Texas Senate voted on a resolution of praise for farm worker organizer Cesar Chavez, he wrote,

It makes me realize how true is the old saying, "No man's life or property is safe when the legislature is in session."

Cesar Chavez's terror tactics easily match those of the oldtime night riders in the South. Incidentally, he's the one man I've ever known who can go on a fast and gain weight.

When a psychiatrist said publicly that Reagan's statements on California mental health care demonstrate that the governor was "under strain," Reagan was unconcerned:

Well, you know a head shrinker. He's probably sitting there right now looking at the pupils of my eyes on television. He can see me on a couch. Well I want to tell you if I get on a couch it will be to take a nap.

Under [federal] regulations, for example, in Connecticut a sixth grade boy's choir, long a tradition in the community, was forced to disband because it violated the HEW guidelines against sex discrimination. They say that musical groups can only be divided now on a basis of vocal range; but in the sixth grade the boys still sing soprano!

During a college demonstration when students chanted around the governor's limousine, "We are the future," Reagan scribbled a reply on a piece of paper, which he held up to the car window:

I'll sell my bonds.

Noticing that there was a large amount of official stationery remaining from the previous administration of Gov. Pat Brown, Reagan asked his secretary, in the interest of fiscal responsibility,

Couldn't we just X out his name?

1967

Regarding that tax increase—I feel like the mother spanking her lovable but recalcitrant child—it hurt me more than it hurt you.

San Francisco, Calif.
March 6, 1968

When a young man suggested that the governor would establish better relations with the younger generation if he rode a motorcycle, Reagan respectfully declined:

I . . . think I'll have to stick to horseback riding. You see, there is the matter of security. When I go anyplace, I'm one of a group. We might look like Hell's Angels with all of us out there on motorcycles.

Mindful of the fact that the Democratic Speaker of the California Assembly, Jesse Unruh, had reduced from 285 to 200 pounds, Governor Reagan commented,

It seems like it takes more than a tailor to change the image of Big Daddy.

A senate committee set up a distinguished research team, headed by a prestigious professor, who discovered that if you cut bus fares in half, more people would ride the bus. They got so excited about their discovery, they pursued it and learned you can further increase patronage if you pay people a dime to ride the bus. And even more people will ride if you pay them twenty cents. But then they had to report failure. They discovered that even when you pay people, you cannot get 100 percent use of rapid transit. This is my kind of sneaky way of telling that sixty million Americans still drive to work each day and we will be supporting new highways for years to come.

September 8, 1972

When government uses its coercive power to intervene in the free marketplace, agriculture can discover it has something worse to contend with than the corn borer or the boll weevil.

December 11, 1972

I had a nightmare last night; I dreamed I owned a Laundromat in Berkeley.

1970

Government does not solve problems; it subsidizes them.

December 11, 1972

Letter to Nelson Rockefeller:

Dear Nelson:

Thanks very much for the autographed copy of your book, which I found awaiting me. I'm looking forward to reading it just as soon as I can get about 600 d——n bills signed, most of which could be left unsigned with great benefit to the people of Calif.

I'll see you in Miami. Again thanks.

Best regards,

Ron

1968

I've got a new way to stop smog. Stop burning down schools.

Labor Day 1970

Too many people, especially in government, feel that the nearest thing to eternal life we will ever see on this earth is a government program.

May 10, 1972

Americans have had their night on the town of social tinkering and social experimentation. They are now suffering the morning after, and they are hungry for some good old ham and eggs fiscal common sense.

The young people want three political parties—one in power, one out of power, and one marching on Sacramento.

Labor Day 1970

Reagan likes to talk about the difficulties he encountered soon after assuming the governorship:

I tried to dial a prayer and they hung up on me!

1967

You might be weary of me sounding the same alarms. You might think, well, we have heard all this before, but somehow we muddled through. Well, this is like the window-washer who fell from the Empire State Building. When he passed the twentieth floor, he said, "So far, so good."

October 29, 1972

In some dim beginning, man created the institution of government as a convenience for himself. And ever since that time, government has been doing its best to become an inconvenience. Government bureaus and agencies take on a life and a purpose of their own. But I wonder if it happens because so many of us—all of us probably—read and hear and just repeat what we think is a truism: that when a public problem develops, government is forced to step in. That is utter nonsense. Government can hardly wait to step in. As a matter of fact, government is in the position of the fellow who will make a speech at the drop of a hat.

Before U.S. Chamber of Commerce
September 24, 1972

58

I think, regardless of who the [presidential] candidate is on the Democratic side, we [Republicans] have to take them very seriously, because we are a minority party, we're outnumbered. Having been a Democrat for a great part of my life—until I progressed and learned more—I know how difficult it is to get someone to leave his party and vote the other ticket. So I always run a little scared.

July 14, 1972

Commenting about the speed with which the press began to attack the new Reagan administration, the governor said:

I had been led to believe there was a honeymoon period, but evidently I lost the license on the way to church.

1967

When prodded by a reporter who wanted to know if Reagan actually had sold property he owned in Riverside County, California, Reagan replied:

Are you offering to buy, because I'm willing to sell?

When his daughter Maureen reported that she had been to South Vietnam with a Hollywood troupe and thought that a military victory was not possible, Reagan commented,

Well, now, while I'm partial to my daughter and love her very much, I don't think foreign policy should be decided by USO entertainers.

About welfare, the governor commented,

I fear that with the best of intentions, with only a desire to help those less fortunate, we are making a god of government. A Samaritan crossed over the road and helped the beaten pilgrim himself—he did not report the case to the nearest welfare agency.

After being briefed about California's vast and complex water system, the governor smiled,

I guess there's more to it than lying down by the creek and drinking your belly full.

Correspondence between John Wayne and Reagan:

Honorable Ronald Reagan
1341 45th Street
Sacramento, Calif.

Dear Ronnie:

Working like hell here at Fort Benning in the great state of Georgia.

The peaches have lost their fuzz, the frost is on the pumpkin, and we're working nights.

I read the enclosed article by Paul Harvey regarding your clear thinking and articulate manner in explaining same. It was refreshing to read something so aptly expressed. Thank God for Harvey, and keep up the good work, friend.

Love to Nancy.

Sincerely,

John Wayne

                                        October 10, 1967

Mr. John Wayne
Camellia Motel
Columbus, Georgia

Dear Duke:

It was good to hear from you and thanks so much for sending the article. I'll keep it around as a chaser for some of those *Los Angeles Times* editorials.

I was in South Carolina last week, and if you hear a

rumor that we're not well acquainted, I played down our friendship to get out of roping you into a benefit. Some people corraled me, had it all set up to fly you in and out of location in a Piper Cub I think, if I'd only get on the phone and urge you to do their benefit. I said I didn't think our relationship was close enough for me to do such a thing. I couldn't think of any other way of not calling you.

Nancy sends her love and I hope we'll be seeing you soon.

Best regards,

Sincerely,

Ronald Reagan
Governor

To set the record straight that he had never said "If you've seen one redwood, you've seen them all," but rather had stated, "A tree is a tree. How many more do you have to look at?" Reagan told reporters,

Some of my best friends are redwoods.

I am opposed [to the legalization of marijuana]. And I am opposed because the score is not in yet [on the medical effects of its use]. The thing I think most people don't realize about legalization of marijuana is that fourteen companies have already registered trade names for marijuana cigarettes. Once you make them legal, you're going to see billboards, and packs in the vending machines. Since marijuana is smoked for effect—not for the taste, as cigarettes—how are they going to advertise? What are they going to say—"Fly higher with ours"?

Before members of Boys State
Sacramento, Calif.
June 22, 1972

When Reagan had to leave the state briefly, he left a note for his lieutenant governor, Robert Finch:

Dear Bob:

Solve something.

Ron

P.S. Solve anything.

Although he discussed his military career in his autobiography, Where's the Rest of Me? *a letter to the* San Francisco Chronicle *made some errors regarding his time in the army. Reagan wrote back,*

One thing the letters have proven is that my book, *Where's the Rest of Me?* was not a bestseller. That's strange, too, because it is the best book I've ever written—it is also the only book I've ever written.

1972

We sure can't be like the fellow's wife who used to cut off both ends of the ham before she cooked it. When he asked her why she did that, she said because that's the way her mother always did it.

One day, he got the chance to ask his mother-in-law why she cut off both ends of the ham before she cooked it. And she said because that's the way her mother did it.

Came the holidays and Grandma was visiting and he told her about it and asked if that was true—why did she cut off both ends of the ham before she cooked it? She said, "That's simple. I never had a pan big enough to get the whole ham in it."

May 31, 1974

If the Interstate Commerce Commission had been in business during the pioneer days, the 49ers would still be trying to find out what the rules are for crossing the Mississippi River.

October 15, 1974

During the Symbionese Liberation Army's rudimentary food distribution program in California, the governor quipped,

It's too bad we can't have an epidemic of botulism.

1974

We've heard a great deal about Republican fat cats—how the Republicans are the party of big contributions. I've never been able to understand why a Republican contributor is a fat cat and a Democratic contributor of the same amount of money is a public-spirited philanthropist.

At Republican fundraiser
Los Angeles, Calif.
August 4, 1974

The Republican Party is more in tune with the thinking of the majority of the American people than is the other major party or either of the splinter parties that started up. I do not believe that for vote-getting purposes you go out and vitiate, water down your true philosophical beliefs in order to persuade someone to vote for you. The Democrats have been doing things like that for years and that's why they have got a weird coalition that can't enjoy itself in one room together.

News conference
Sacramento, Calif.
November 12, 1974

If I have dwelt overlong on troubles besetting all of us before getting to those peculiar to California and California's government, it was to guard against the experience of a

63

gentleman who departed this earth from a point somewhere in western Pennsylvania. Arriving at the Pearly Gates he was greeted by St. Peter and given an indoctrination course, during which he learned the heavenly oldtimers had a story-telling ring and were particularly interested in newcomers who might have interesting earthly experiences to relate. He told St. Peter he was a cinch to go over big—he was the sole survivor in his town of the Johnstown flood. Peter took him over to the group and gave him a flattering intro-duction and buildup. The Pennsylvanian stepped forward to begin his exciting story. At which point, Peter murmured in his ear: "By the way, that old guy in the front row is a fellow named Noah."

Speech to Economic Club
New York, N.Y.
January 17, 1968

From those first few years when I kept you posted on how much we were saving on typewriter ribbons, these meetings have come to be an opportunity for me to report on the state of the state.

It is a pleasure to do so, especially this year because our fiscal situation is considerably improved and so are a few other things.

For example, last year when we met, the legislature was still in session. This year, they are still in session, but they have gone home for a while. The script is like one of those long-running soap operas on daytime TV.

Will Laura give up Mickey for Bill?

Will Bill find happiness with Cynthia?

Will there be action on tax reform and school finance?

Will they protect the environment without declaring the state off limits to people?

Will they ever start going home again on June 30?

Tune in next November.

Transcript of remarks by
Gov. Ronald Reagan
Sacramento Host Breakfast
September 8, 1972

Some political figures have endured in history as lions or conquerors or something equally impressive. It's a little frightening to think California history might record us as jellybeans.

1974

5.
THE
YEARS
IN
BETWEEN

During the years he neither held office nor was a candidate, Reagan had considerable time to reflect on his career and future. He also had the opportunity to examine the nation and speak with Americans around the country. While the world and America and, to a certain extent, Ronald Reagan were changing, his sense of humor remained intact. His wit survived the governorship and especially the problems at Berkeley. What emerged was a man who could still laugh at himself with style.

In the business that I used to be in, you learn not to stay on stage too long. You learn there's a time you have to exit.

Evansville, Ind.
September 24, 1978

When asked by a reporter whether he might run against Jimmy Carter for President in 1980, Reagan said that Carter remained "kind of a mystery" to him and that the former Georgia governor was a "hard target."

I've never seen anyone throw a peanut in the air and shoot it.

Evansville, Ind.
September 24, 1978

Commenting to British exporters:

I was surprised you hadn't retaliated for some of the movies we sent you. But lately I've been listening to some of the records bought by our children and I think you're beginning to get even.

In my job these past eight years I've been a part of big-time education as a regent of the University of California—all nine campuses and more than 100,000 students. All I've seen since has convinced me if I had it to do over again, I'd still go to Eureka. Just being elbowed in a crowd as 27,000 students go milling between classes isn't necessarily where the action is.

On the fact that Republicans have never had much electoral appeal in times of economic stress:

For forty years or more this country has been following the lute song of the liberals. Suddenly, when they come undone with their planned economy, their deficit spending, and their deliberately planned inflation, which they said would maintain prosperity, how the hell do the conservatives get blamed?

Criticizing strict government controls on business:

We have all heard that if you build a better mousetrap, the world would beat a path to your door. Today if you build a better mousetrap, the government comes along with a better mouse.

Cullman, Ala.
March 21, 1975

On the Carter administration's foreign policy:

Internationally, they don't seem to know the difference between being a diplomat and a doormat. Take, for example, our approach to the . . . SALT talks, the refusal to ac-knowledge that the Soviet Union is building the greatest war machine known to man. Somehow, we've negotiated agreements [under which] we grow weaker and they grow stronger.

Interview
Los Angeles, Calif.
December 12, 1977

Our problem isn't a shortage of fuel, it's a surplus of government.

Having been a Democrat most of my life, I know how hard it is to mark that ballot the other way. It's almost like changing religions.

1978

I don't have much faith in the third-party movement. I think a third party usually succeeds in electing the people they set out to oppose.

Broadcast interview
San Francisco, Calif.
August 29, 1975

Commenting on the victory of Democrat Jimmy Carter, Reagan said,

For the first time, the Democrats cannot fuzz up the issue by blaming the White House. They've got the whole enchilada now.

Politics is supposed to be the second oldest profession. I have come to realize that it bears a very close resemblance to the first.

At a business conference
Los Angeles, Calif.
March 2, 1977

In show business we used to say that if you don't sing or dance, you wind up an after-dinner speaker.

1979

Maybe the trouble with those professional women's libbers I mentioned earlier is related to something Will Rogers once said, "If women go on trying to be more and more equal to men, some day they won't know any more than men do."

1976

6.
REAGAN
LOOKS
AT
REAGAN

A person can be funny in many instances while lacking wit or a sense of humor. What gives a person these qualities is the ability to cast laughter over oneself, to take pot shots at one's own failings and mistakes, to admit error or defeat with a bit more than a smile. Indeed, it is this capability that inspires leadership.

Much of Ronald Reagan's wit is directed toward himself. His images of the world and himself are equally realistic and amusing. When he swallows his pride, he does so with a shot of quicksilver; the result is often more than the usual Reagan quip. By no other way can we better understand this fascinating and remarkable man than reading what he has to say about himself. The anecdotes, witticisms, and stories in this chapter come from all periods of the career of Ronald Reagan.

Reagan wrote in his autobiography,

The story begins with a closeup of a bottom. My face was blue from screaming, my bottom was red from whacking, and my father claimed afterward he was white when he said shakily, "For such a little bit of a fat Dutchman, he makes a hell of a lot of noise, doesn't he?"

Ever since my birth my nickname has been "Dutch" and I have been particularly fond of the colors that were exhibited—red, white and blue. I have not been uncomfortable on the various occasions when I have had an overwhelming impulse to brandish them.

I became the first Errol Flynn of the B's. I was as brave as Errol, but in a low-budget fashion.

1965

I have heard more than one psychiatrist say that we imbibe our ideals from our mother's milk. Then, I must say, my breast feeding was the home of the brave baby and the free bosom. I was the hungriest person in the house but I only got chubby when I exercised in the crib; any time I wasn't gnawing on the bars, I was worrying with my thumb in my mouth—habits which have symbolically persisted throughout my life.

1965

There is no foundation to the rumor that I am the only one here who was at the original Al Smith dinner.

At 35th annual Al Smith Dinner
New York, N.Y.

During a Republican debate for the 1980 nomination, Reagan remarked that wage and price controls had continually failed since the time of the Roman emperor Diocletian. He added:

I'm the only one here old enough to remember.

1980

When the famous San Francisco attorney Jake Ehrlich asked Governor Reagan to autograph a picture of the two of them taken some twenty years earlier, Reagan wrote back,

I have just received your photograph, and am certain it is a fake. We were never that young.

Nature was trying to tell me something. Namely, my heart is a hamloaf.

I loved three things: drama, politics, and sports, and I'm not sure they always came in that order.

1965

74

During the primary race, candidate Reagan complained to reporters that they were incorrectly fashioning

the notion that [in my films] I never got the girl in the end. In fact, I was usually the steady, sincere suitor—the one the girl finally turned to.

1980

I was born in a small town in the Midwest, and I was in poverty before the rich folks got hold of it.

1965

When Newsweek *reported that Reagan wore pancake makeup, Reagan denied it in a letter to the editor in which he said he never wore it offstage or onstage:*

You see, when I was younger, I could get along without it. And now it wouldn't help any.

1966

Holding out a glass of tonic water, Reagan demonstrated his youthfulness:

I feel just fine. Look, not even a ripple.

1979

I was a near hopeless hemophilic liberal.

1947

In a letter to the editor of a college paper, he wrote,

Please tell Miss Marcus that I wore no makeup at the Commonwealth Club (I'm allergic to it). In the interest of press integrity also tell her she has a standing invitation to do a "white glove" test on my face the next time she is assigned to cover an appearance of mine!

I'm not smart enough to lie.

July 1980

While visiting a construction site, Reagan told workers that the hard hat they offered him would not fit because,

I have a pinhead.

October 1980

Citing Thomas Jefferson's advice not to worry about one's age, Reagan said,

Ever since he told me that, I stopped worrying.

1981

Commenting on his average acting career, Reagan said,

I'm no Flynn or Boyer. Mr. Norm is my alias.

I think I'm kind of moderate. Maybe we can overdo moderation.

1980

As the President-elect, Reagan reflected,

I remember some of my own views when I was quite young. For heaven's sake, I was even a Democrat.

1980

Apologizing to some aides for being late, Reagan said,

The only reason I'm late, is that I had to oil my face.

February 1981

When asked to autograph a picture from his film Bedtime for Bonzo, *which showed Ronald Reagan and the chimpanzee in bed together, Reagan wrote,*

I'm the one with the watch.

I don't think it [age] is important. Samuel Colt invented the revolver when he was twenty, and Verdi wrote *Falstaff* when he was eighty. I'm somewhere in between. There are days when the legislature is especially busy and I feel older than Verdi—and days when I feel like Colt.

August 22, 1972

There are those who will say having me here as speaker is a perfect job of typecasting. You are staging a celebration in the style and atmosphere of the last century. Some people would go even farther where I'm concerned and suggest that I belong to the Ice Age.

Columbus, Ga.
July 4, 1968

In spite of Jack's curse, I was not a teetotaler. Like almost every other young man, I had learned to drink—principally because it was against the law—and it was done out of a bottle that tasted like gasoline on the fraternity back porch or in a parked car.

When a woman gave Reagan an old autographed photograph of younger Ronald Reagan, the candidate sighed,

You sent this to me. I was never that young.

March 1980

7.
THE
CAMPAIGN
FOR
PRESIDENT: 1976

Although he came close, Reagan lost the Republican nomination for President in 1976. But during the months of active campaigning, Reagan's wit was in full form. His humor was directed mainly toward the federal government, and had the government been his opponent for the nomination, he certainly would have won.

The government in Washington is spending some $7 million every minute I talk to you. There's no connection between my talking and their spending, and if they'll stop spending, I'll stop talking.

May 1976

When asked whether he thought the presidency should be limited to a single term, Reagan remarked,

There has been talk about a single-year sentence—er, term. . . . You can see I have no illusions about the job.

May 1976

It's been said that if you put [President] Ford and me together in a darkroom, you can't tell us apart philosophically. Well, if you turn on the light, you can.

May 1976

After having been asked about his position on the Panama Canal for the umpteenth time, Reagan quipped:

If they don't watch out, I'll come out and start defending the Erie Canal.

May 1976

As his prospects grew, so did the number and difficulty of the questions posed to him by reporters:

Where before they were just nibbling around the edges, they come in biting now.

January 1976

Quoting Bismarck, Reagan quipped,

If you like laws and sausages, you should never watch either one being made.

Oklahoma City, Okla.
June 4, 1976

If you would render all the fat in government, you'd have enough soap to wash the world.

January 1975

Bureaucrats favor cutting red tape—lengthwise.

November 1975

Defending his vice presidential running mate, Reagan said that Senator Schweiker

has not become a captive of what I call the Washington buddy system.

July 1976

About the paper generated by the federal bureaucracy, Reagan observed,

Wouldn't it make a great annual bonfire?

February 1976

I think we have two groups of [environmental] extremists. There are, of course, those people on one side who would pave the country over in the name of progress. There is an extremist group on the other extreme that wouldn't let you build a house unless it looked like a bird's nest. Now, I think there has to be a commonsense in-between that recognizes the people are ecology, too.

August 1976

Professional politicians like to talk about the value of experience in government. Nuts! The only experience you gain in politics is how to be political.

1976

Reagan opposes busing schoolchildren, but he did support

busing some of the bureaucrats in Washington out into the country to meet the real people.

February 1976

Reagan is firmly opposed to government handouts to business:

This is feeding the crocodile in hopes he will eat you last, but eat you he will.

February 1976

Reagan remarked that the only benefit of detente for the U.S. has been the acquisition of the right to sell Pepsi-Cola in Siberia.

February 1976

Any candidate who says he isn't frightened is a liar or a fool.

Oklahoma City, Okla.
June 4, 1976

8.
THE
CAMPAIGN
FOR
PRESIDENT: 1980

The opportunities for wit and humor were as numerous as the campaign issues and his opponents for President. Reagan took full advantage of these primary campaigns and the general election to jest and reveal exactly how potent his wit is. One by one, Reagan defeated his fellow contenders for the Republican nomination and then went on to captivate the American people.

Americans followed the campaign with a realization that the result of this election would be of great importance for them as individuals and for the nation. They eagerly anticipated the smooth Reagan wit. Even though the primary races were grueling and marked with anxiety and occasional bitterness, Reagan saved his wit for attacks on the Democrats, preferring to leave his Republican Party unscathed.

When his microphone began to fail, Reagan said,

Why do I have the feeling that I'm fading out? [Vice President] Mondale isn't in the city by any chance, is he?

Chicago, Ill.
October 31, 1980

I haven't had Jimmy Carter's experience. I wouldn't be caught dead with it.

1980

When President Carter and Ronald Reagan were both campaigning in Columbus, Ohio, on the same day, Reagan told his supporters,

I heard some people are having trouble telling which motorcade is which. Well, his turns left at every corner.

Columbus, Ohio
1980

Reagan told supporters that the President "promised tax increases" when he wanted to say "decreases." He explained,

I've been talking about Carter so long that I make mistakes like he does.

Grand Rapids, Mich.
November 1, 1980

When it was reported that President Carter forecast better economic times, Reagan retorted,

I don't know what country he was talking about.

Cleveland, Ohio
May 30, 1980

Asked how he thought he fared after the debate with President Carter, Reagan replied,

It seemed to go all right. I've examined myself and I can't find any wounds.

November 1980

In place of imagination, Mr. Carter calls for more government regulation. In place of ingenuity, he calls for more federal guidelines.

Sunnyvale, Calif.
September 25, 1980

An Annapolis graduate may be at the helm of the ship of state, but it has no rudder.

Criticizing his Democratic opponent, President Carter, Reagan said,

Maybe it's about time we had a President who remembered the Great Depression and what it was all about.

Birmingham, Mich.
October 16, 1980

In response to finding out that he had been endorsed by staunch liberal Eugene McCarthy, Reagan said,

Maybe this will give some people confidence that I don't eat my young.

1980

Depression is when you're out of work. A recession is when your neighbor's out of work. Recovery is when Carter's out of work.

1980

When bothered by hecklers, Reagan told his audience,

I hope my mike can outlast their bullhorns.

And when it did not, he showed his displeasure with their shouting and singing:

You know, they can't even sing.

Claremont, Calif.
October 13, 1980

In a remark to his fellow westerners, Reagan quipped,

Let's turn the sagebrush rebellion into a sagebrush solution.

Grand Junction, Colo.
September 23, 1980

Commenting on some of President Carter's charges, Reagan said,

The President is determined to have me start a nuclear war. Well, I'm just as determined that I'm not going to.
October 10, 1980

After his overwhelming victory in the South Carolina primary, Reagan told reporters,

I have been telling some of you that I'm cautiously optimistic. Now I'm cautiously ecstatic.

On a campaign bus in snowy New Hampshire, Reagan quipped:

If anyone hears dogs barking, it's because the next leg will be done by sled.

After his victory in the New Hampshire primary, Reagan told the press,

You fellas are going to call me whatever you want to call me, but I have a hunch it's going to be "front runner."

Reagan confided to an aide about rival George Bush:

I never feel comfortable around him. Whenever he talks to me, he seems to be staring at my necktie.

Yes, the mighty music of American economic progress has been all but silenced for four years of Mr. Carter's failures.
Nationwide TV address
October 24, 1980

When a reporter asked if Reagan had watched the Roger Mudd interview with Senator Kennedy, he replied,

Nancy and I were so tired last night, we watched from bed and fell asleep.

Because of hectic scheduling, Reagan appeared a little overdressed at a Virginia farmhouse:

I'm sorry I'm not dressed the way I should be for a party like this, but I have to run off to Washington—although I counted on doing that more along January.

Middleburg, Va.
September 13, 1980

Alluding to the President's troubles with his brother Billy and the Libyan government, Reagan pointed out that U.S. oil imports had increased from this unstable country:

Maybe he should send more relatives over there.

Cleveland, Ohio
September 10, 1980

When asked about the President's accusation that Reagan was a "traveling salesman" for the American Medical Association, the former governor quipped,

Well, that's better than what he's been peddling.

I think Carter is very vulnerable on his record. To hear him talk about energy and inflation, you'd think someone else had been in charge the last three years.

Reagan invented his own Eleventh Commandment:

Thou shalt not criticize other Republicans.

89

And, later a twelfth:

Thou shalt not be overconfident.

July 1980

When reporters asked candidate Reagan to respond to President Carter's charge that Reagan proposed military solutions to various diplomatic problems, he said,

You fellows have heard about everything I've said. Have you ever heard me say that? I'll bet none of you ever have because I've never said it.

Pensacola, Fla.
September 23, 1980

The next time you go to the supermarket and see that astronomical number on the little white piece of paper, just remember that Mr. Carter told you not to worry about fluctuations.

Pensacola, Fla.
September 23, 1980

Reagan charged that President Carter, at a press conference,

stood there with his bare face hanging out and said the inflation rate was going to stay in the single-digit level. How can it stay where it hasn't been and isn't now?

Ft. Lauderdale, Fla.
September 22, 1980

I am what I have always been, and I intend to remain that way.

November 1, 1980

When interrupted by a heckler, Reagan responded:

Aw, shut up.

After his supporters cheered and applauded, Reagan went on,

My mother always told me I should never say that, but I heard so many like him and this is the last day of the campaign and I thought for just once I could say it.

San Diego, Calif.
November 3, 1980

Reagan said that the President had failed because of

his total inability to fill Jerry Ford's shoes.

Grand Rapids, Mich.
November 1, 1980

Speaking in Los Angeles, Reagan joked,

Nancy and I have been so homesick, campaigning all over the East, that we would be happy to be here, even in the smog siege.

October 13, 1980

My opponent would have you believe that instead of campaigning, I have been out starting nuclear wars.

St. Louis, Mo.
1980

Talking to farmers, Reagan said,

If government payments were made on the basis of damage done by government, farmers all over America would be collecting disaster payments.

Nevada, Iowa
September 29, 1980

*After President Carter changed his campaign tactics, and
made the current issues the primary focus, Reagan said,*

I'm glad to see he's going to straighten up and fly right.
Trevose, Pa.
1980

You know, I think the best possible social program is
a job.
Trevose, Pa.
1980

*When asked whether he thought President Carter had pro-
vided an adequate explanation for his brother Billy's actions
regarding Libya, Reagan said,*

Well, he does seem to be dragging his feet.
Pittsburgh, Pa.
1980

I had a dream the other night. I dreamed that Jimmy
Carter came to me and asked why I wanted his job. I told
him I didn't want his job. I want to be President.
Detroit, Mich.
July 14, 1980

Carter was supposed to go on "60 Minutes" to talk
about his accomplishments, but that left him with 59 minutes
to fill.
Middleburg, Va.
September 13, 1980

Carter couldn't get the Russians to move out of Cuba
so he's moving out the Cubans.
Middleburg, Va.
September 13, 1980

We now know what Mr. Carter plans to do with four more years. Catch your breath, hold onto your hats, and grab your wallets because Jimmy Carter's analysis of the economy means that his answer is higher taxes.

Lima, Ohio
October 15, 1980

After lamenting the 58 percent increase in government spending during the Carter administration, Reagan asked,

How many of you were able to increase your spending by 58 percent in the last four years? Well, that's how much government spending has gone up.

Houston, Tex.
October 29, 1980

Jimmy Carter's in the White House. Amy's in the treehouse. Billy's in the doghouse.

Topeka, Kan.
October 20, 1980

Reagan gave this explanation of why the President would not join the debate between him and John Anderson:

President Carter has been debating candidate Carter for the past three and a half years—and losing.

Houston, Tex.
September 16, 1980

Commenting on the Carter administration's changing the statistical base of the producer price index, Reagan lamented,

They have taken to making highly questionable uses of official governmental statistics to sugarcoat the bitter pill that has regularly come from Washington in the line of economic news.

Now measured by the way this administration has used the imperial incumbency over the past year, I am not surprised [by] the recent—forgive me for this—"Jimmying" of official governmental statistics. What we need is a change in the economy and not a change in the statistics.

Cherry Hill, N.J.
October 6, 1980

Referring to President Carter, Reagan commented,

He said he'd do something about unemployment. He did. In April, 825,000 Americans lost their jobs.

Cleveland, Ohio
May 30, 1980

Reagan lamented President Carter's relations with Congress:

Pennsylvania Avenue must be a two-way street.

Washington, D.C.
September 15, 1980

Referring to Carter's accusations that Reagan is a warmonger, the former governor responded,

You know, in spite of what the President has said, I've never had my thumb on the button once.

1980

When someone shouted "I want Teddy" at a Reagan rally, Reagan quipped,

There's a fella back there who wants Teddy—he's sick.

San Diego, Calif.
June 2, 1980

The President had ordered there be no hard liquor in the White House. And now we find some of the White House has been smoking pot. This is the first administration we can honestly say is high and dry.

Topeka, Kan.
October 29, 1980

Reagan was spotted reading a New York Times *analysis of his latest foreign policy speech:*

I want to see what these bastards are saying so I can protect myself. You can sure tell when you're in hostile territory.

1980

Referring to easterners' impressions of him, Reagan said,

Horns begin to grow as soon as I cross the Mississippi.

April 1980

Hell, I could have campaigned on the same things he campaigned on. The only difference was he forgot them between Plains and Washington.

1980

When disrupted by hecklers, Reagan said,

At some point back there, those who deny the rights of others to speak who don't share their particular views were raising their hands in a salute more familiar in my younger days. They were saying, "Heil, Reagan." Well you know, I take a little pride, if you'll pardon me, in the fact that if it wasn't for my generation, they'd be saying, "Heil, somebody," today.

Huntington Beach, Calif.
October 13, 1980

Reagan said that President Carter's Middle East policy

zigzags and flipflops in ever more rapid gyrations, trying to court favor with everyone.

Washington, D.C.
September 3, 1980

Asked by an Iowa farmer if he was concerned about rising farm-land prices, Reagan replied,

Not when I sell, but when I buy.

September 31, 1980

We started with an administration that didn't have any plan, any economic plan, of what they were going to do with the presidency other than enjoy it. And now we're reaping this harvest, and I look forward to turning around some of the things that have gone wrong.

Chicago, Ill.
October 30, 1980

Talking about his opponent, Reagan remarked,

The reason he is so obsessed with poverty is that he never had any as a kid.

Chicago, Ill.
October 31, 1980

Speaking to Democrats, the candidate said,

I know what it's like to pull the Republican lever for the first time, because I used to be a Democrat myself, and I can tell you it only hurts for a minute and then it feels just great.

Bayonne, N.J.
October 25, 1980

96

When Reagan told a crowd of supporters that the litany of Carter's economic excuses "makes you wonder who's been in charge for the last three and a half years," his audience shouted back, "Amy! Amy!"—a reference to the President's remark that his daughter had told him that nuclear proliferation was the uppermost issue on her mind. Reagan then added,

That could be. I know he touched our hearts, all of us, the other night. I remember when Patti and Ron were little tiny kids we used to talk about nuclear power.

Milwaukee, Wis.
October 1980

It isn't always necessary to make [legislators] see the light, as long as you can make them feel the heat.

1980

After complaining about the mountains of undesired forms sent to citizens by the government, Reagan noticed photographers firing off picture after picture of him rolling an orange:

You could send them out instead of forms.

Milwaukee, Wis.
October 1980

Referring to President Carter, Reagan said that he had

taken refuge behind a dictionary.

1980

The conduct of the presidency under Mr. Carter has become a tragic comedy of errors. In place of competence, he has given us ineptitude. Instead of steadiness, we have gotten vacillation. While America looks for confidence, he

97

gives us fear. His multitude of promises so richly pledged in 1976 have fallen by the wayside in the shambles of this administration.

Texarkana, Ark.
October 29, 1980

Reagan was asked by a reporter to comment on a remark by pollster Lou Harris, who said that because Reagan had done well in the debate with President Carter, the election was now Reagan's to lose.

Well, I'll tell you that if Lou Harris says the election is mine to lose, the best thing for me to do is stop talking to you people.

He then grinned and added,

I'm only kidding.

New Orleans, La.
October 29, 1980

No one should feel any obligation to reward his four years of total mismanagement with four more years to do the very same. He did not give us a government as good as the people, as he said he would do. He only gave us a government as good as Jimmy Carter, and that isn't good enough.

New Orleans, La.
October 29, 1980

Referring to his Democratic opponent, Reagan lamented,

When I look at what he has done in the past four years, you can see why he spent so little time last night in the debate talking about his record. He has grown fond of referring to Franklin Roosevelt, Harry Truman, and John Kennedy. There's one Democratic president he doesn't talk about, and that's Jimmy Carter. To hear him talk, you would

98

think someone else had been in charge for the last four years.

Houston, Tex.
October 29, 1980

Candidate Reagan warned that the President would

continue to take us into the economic dark ages.

Lima, Ohio
October 15, 1980

When told that in a poll Congressman John Anderson had outpointed him on their nationally televised debate, Reagan commented,

How come I still feel so good?

Pensacola, Fla.
September 23, 1980

Reagan had some thoughts on Carter's statement "I will never lie to you":

After hearing that line about twenty times I was reminded of Ralph Waldo Emerson's line, "The louder he talked of his honor, the faster we counted our spoons."

Jacksonville, Fla.
September 4, 1980

I've been very busy, as you know, starting nuclear wars and doing away with social security and all those things—that is, if you listen to what the other fellas are saying.

1980

No matter how much he tries to run away from his record, he has to account for it to the American people.

Des Plaines, Ill.
October 31, 1980

Referring to the President's charges that Reagan was out to destroy America and the world, Reagan quipped,

You know, after you've canceled social security and started the war, what else is there for you to do?

Milwaukee, Wis.
October 1980

First we must overcome something the present administration has cooked up: a new and altogether indigestible economic stew, one part inflation, one part high unemployment, one part recession, one part runaway taxes, one part deficit spending and seasoned by an energy crisis. It's an economic stew that has turned the national stomach. It is as if Mr. Carter had set out to prove, once and for all, that economics is indeed a "dismal science."

1980

During the debate with President Carter, Reagan remarked,

But when I quoted a Democratic President, as the President says, I was a Democrat. I said many foolish things back in those days.

October 1980

Reagan called President Carter's economic plan:

Quicksilver economics.

Cherry Hill, N.J.
October 6, 1980

100

During the debate with President Carter, Reagan said,

I know the President's supposed to be replying to me, but sometimes I have a hard time in connecting what he's saying with what I have said my positions are. I sometimes think he's like the witch doctor that gets mad when a good doctor comes along with a cure that'll work.

October 1980

The President said I'm irresponsible. Well, I'll admit to being irresponsible if he'll admit to being responsible [for some of the nation's problems].

Des Plaines, Ill.
October 31, 1980

You know, now that I have a farm they send me the Sears catalog. And I must confess I'm impressed. There's such a wide variety of consumer products available through that one company; we ought to send every Russian a Sears catalog.

During their debate, Reagan asked his opponent, John Anderson,

John, would you *really* find Teddy Kennedy preferable to me?

I'm saying the same things I've been saying for twenty-five years on the mashed-potato circuit. So is a preacher in church on Sunday.

9.
THE
PRESIDENCY

When he finally achieved the goal for which he had worked for over a decade, Reagan quipped, "I guess I can go back to California, can't I?" But for Ronald Reagan, the oldest President in our nation's history and the only one to have been a member of both major parties, there was no turning back to the halcyon days of Sacramento. In a decade of unprecedented social and technological change, a man with an unwavering set of values and principles had become President of the United States.

From the first few moments of his presidency, Reagan's wit illuminated his administration, helping to soften the rough spots that always accompany a new President. Through his humor Reagan soon became known as one of the most amiable Presidents, and certainly among the wittiest. During the first 100 days of his administration, Reagan's wit was an energetic force behind his programs and proposals. That wit provides a window through which to view our President and how he deals with his office and the world.

The President-elect felt that it was important to meet as many members of Congress as possible. He later observed,

I've been smiling so much my jowls hurt.

1980

At a luncheon for Republican senators and congressmen, the President-elect decided to keep his remarks brief:

If I keep on with this, I'll be making a campaign speech, and I don't want to do that.

1980

Shortly before assuming the office of President of the United States, Reagan was briefed by his advisers on the many problems facing America. Reagan quipped,

I think I'll demand a recount!

At a press conference a reporter prefaced his question by saying, "Mr. President, I'd like to get back to El Salvador for a second." Retorted Reagan,

Do we have to?

Washington, D.C.
March 6, 1981

At a meeting with his cabinet and overzealous budget director David Stockman, the group quickly approved a mere $125 million reduction in Department of Energy administration costs. Fearing Stockman would have more to cut, Reagan asked for comments, and hearing none, immediately said,

Good! All right. Turn the page quick.

Washington, D.C.
February 1981

When told that President Kennedy assessed the presidency this way, "The pay is pretty good and you can walk home to lunch," Reagan quipped,

Oh? I've been here two days and I've had lunch both days in this office.

Washington, D.C.
January 22, 1981

Soon after the inauguration the festivities died down, and Ronald Reagan settled into his role as President of the United States.

Good morning all—a good morning without the marine band. It's very quiet getting down here.

Washington, D.C.
January 23, 1981

Speaking to the White House Correspondents Association, Reagan told reporters,

Mark Twain is supposed to have said there's nothing harder to put up with than the annoyance of a good example, and you certainly have been that to the White House press corps.

Camp David, Md.
April 25, 1981

Remarks of the President at dinner honoring Secretary Block by the National Association of State Departments of Agriculture:

I learned in public speaking you're never supposed to open with an apology, but my schedule has kind of gotten jammed up with two things happening almost simultaneously so I only have a few minutes. But I did want to come here and, first of all, thank you and commend you for whom you selected to honor tonight, Secretary of Agriculture John Block and his lovely lady.

You know, I have to tell you this has been quite a day. I had lunch at the Irish embassy. It happened to be an appropriate occasion for that today. And before I left—it's the most infectious brogue in the world. Before I left, I was talking just like, well, you know.

But we've changed gears here and I tried to warn John about some of the things that—I remember when Ezra Taft Benson was secretary of agriculture, and he was out in the country and hearing reports from people in the farm areas and talking to them and at one place, there was a fellow that was giving him a really bad time, really complaining and Ezra turned around and looked at some notes that some-one handed him and then turned back and said, "Now, wait a minute. You didn't have it so bad." He said, "You had twenty-six inches of rain this last year." And the fellow says, "Yes, I remember the night it happened."

All of you are engaged in what is really the energy industry that is the most important of all because the energy you produce, or that you have to do with that is produced, if it isn't, we are out of business. And I know once when I was out on the mashed potato circuit before I—that was when I was unemployed—I was speaking to a farm group in Las Vegas and on the way in to where I was to speak there was one of those fellows that was there for the action and he recognized me. And he said, "What are you doing here?" I told him. He said, "What are a bunch of farmers doing in Las Vegas?" And I just couldn't help it. I said, "Buster, they're in a business that makes a Las Vegas craps table look like a guaranteed annual income."

Washington, D.C.
March 17, 1981

When asked about a second term, Reagan quipped,

Well, you know I never could have achieved welfare reform in California without a second term.

Washington, D.C.
January 22, 1981

The President spoke briefly to the American hostages freed from Iran and to their families:

Now don't get worried. There's not going to be a lengthy speech. I've been in office now for one week and one of the things I've found out is that there are a few orders that I can give. So tonight I am officially ordering that all of you have a good rest, catch up with your families, and as

106

much as Nancy and George and I and Barbara enjoy having you as our guests, we simply don't want to keep you from the privacy that you now deserve.

I know that a great many historic events have happened in this house. There have been many thousands of important people hosted here. But right at this moment I can't think of anyone more distinguished than you. So God bless all of you. Thank you again. Thank you for serving our country, for doing your duty. We're all very happy to have you back where you belong. And we're now going to go and you have just received your second freedom.

Washington, D.C.
January 27, 1981

Speaking about his secretary of the treasury, Donald Regan, the President discovered a class distinction in the two Irishmen's names:

Those who called themselves "Reegan" were the lawyers and doctors. It was only the laborers and the farmers who called themselves "Raygan."

Washington, D.C.
February 1981

After meeting with Speaker of the House Thomas P. O'Neill, Reagan told reporters,

He said I was in the big leagues now.

After pausing a moment, the President added,

I gathered that already

Washington, D.C.
January 22, 1981

Remarks outside Angelo's Restaurant in the Little Italy section of New York City:

Well, that's what we're going to try to do and, as I say, it's really a great pleasure to be here. Between us, we'll all go to work and we'll all try to do it there in Washington. And now they tell me that they're going to take me inside and feed me. And I heard so much last night about how I'm going to be fed, I haven't had any breakfast yet. I've been waiting for this.

New York, N.Y.
March 14, 1981

When a visiting friend from California was ready to return home, a slightly homesick, and cold (it was February), Ronald Reagan said,

Wait until I get my hat. I'll go with you.

Washington, D.C.
February 1981

About the economy, Reagan said,

But it's going to be a tough fight. There are those who would rather get theirs now than cure inflation. They're going to do everything they can to preserve the status quo. And I ask you, after two years of double-digit inflation and economic stagnation, do you really want to keep the status quo? [Shouts of no.]

I didn't think so. *Status quo*, you know, that is Latin for "the mess we're in."

Washington, D.C.
March 16, 1981

I'm a prisoner of my schedule again.

Washington, D.C.
1981

Concerning his working conditions, Reagan pined,

I feel like a bird in a gilded cage.

In some ways working at the White House reminded Reagan of his father's business in Tampico, Illinois:

I'm back living above the store again.

1981

Q: Mr. President, what is your opinion of American companies that now want to resume business with Iran?

My opinion of American companies that want to resume business with Iran? I hope they're going to do it by long distance. We wouldn't want to go back to having just a different cast of characters but the same show going on.

Washington, D.C.
January 29, 1980

During his first day in office, the President wondered if the previous administration left anything for him. He soon found out:

Well, they've left me some paper clips.

Washington, D.C.
January 1981

Referring to the program to push his budget proposals through Congress, Reagan said,

We may not run this like a quarter mile, but we'll run it.

Washington, D.C.
January 1981

Reagan and House Speaker Thomas P. O'Neill were discussing Grover Cleveland and baseball trivia:

> *Reagan*: I have some affection for him. I played Grover Cleveland Alexander in the movies.

> *O'Neill*: Yes, he was one of the fourteen pitchers to win 300 games.

> *Reagan*: Yes, and the 1926 World Series.

Washington, D.C.
January 1981

Remarks of the President at the National Prayer Breakfast:
Thank you very much. Mr. Chairman, Congressman Hefner, and all of you ladies and gentlemen: Nancy and I are delighted to be here and I want to thank you for the day in my life that you recognized in starting off my celebration of my thirty-first anniversary of my thirty-ninth birthday.

Washington, D.C.
February 5, 1981

Swearing-in ceremony of presidential appointees:
Thank you very much. Thank you very much. Please. I want you to know that I don't expect every morning to be greeted by the Marine Band.

January 21, 1981

Remarks of the President with members of the cabinet and their families:

Good morning, all of you. I had thirty or forty minutes of speech but then I just thought, no, never mind. As you know, this was supposed to be a swearing-in but certain branches of the government don't operate as fast as the others, and so there won't be a swearing-in but we'll get the pictures taken. I'm surprised with some of the delay that some of you who are cabinet members, and not yet sworn

110

in in some of the sections we've had, haven't gotten up and said, I don't work here and walked out.

Washington, D.C.
January 22, 1981

After his first day in office, the President said,

It's been a very wonderful day. I guess I can go back to California. Can't I?

January 1981

Remarks of the President upon greeting delegates of the U.S. Senate Youth Program:

Is Charlie Gould here? Where's Charlie? Hey, Charlie, how are you? Well, now you'll make me all homesick again. I'm pleased—I know you've been welcomed and probably several times since you've been here. I'll just add mine to it. You're now in the famous Rose Garden. Now, I have to confess something to you. When I came here to live a couple of weeks ago, I had always thought that the Rose Garden, the whole thing, was roses. I didn't know that it was a grass garden with a few roses along one side. I better not say that to Nancy or she'll get busy with a spade and we'll have them.

For how many of you is this the first visit to Washington? Well, I remember—if you haven't already, I know you will, see all the historic monuments and the places here that should be seen. Have you been to Lincoln's Monument yet? Lincoln's Memorial—you have? Then it won't do me any good to tip you off. I was going to tell you that I learned the first time I was here—someone told me that if you stand on one side of that massive statue and look up at his face, you see the compassion of Lincoln. If you go around to the other side and look, and the artist must have intended this, you see the strength of the man—a difference in his face depending on which side you're standing. But you've been there now. I know they won't want to interrupt the schedule for you to go back. Just take my word for it—it's there.

111

Remarks at the meeting with state legislators and county executives:

Q: One last question. Where are the jellybeans?

Say, they left your table without any? That's unfair. I had a meeting just before coming in here with the gentlemen who are—there they are. Well, all right. I just had a meeting with the people who are providing them. They provided them in California and I should tell you—look at that gallery we've attracted here. I have to say that when I arrived there was a big jar in the middle of the cabinet table, and I didn't say anything, and even this cabinet here was faster than the cabinet had been in California. You should see them going around passing them as they keep right on talking and arguing. As I've said, there's something of character reading you get in there because there's that fellow that every once in a while, while he's picking them out, ones all the same color, one at a time, passing them on. But the man who delivers them just told me, he gave me a message about how properly to eat them. When I told him that I put three or four different colored ones in my mouth at the same time, [he said] they now have a recipe for eating them. You're supposed to put certain colors together and then that will create a new flavor. Like lemon meringue pie or something. I tell you—next thing you know, we'll have an agency regulating the eating of—

February 9, 1981

When Governor James Thompson of Illinois warned the President that some of his colleagues would accept Reagan's budget cuts over their dead bodies, Reagan quipped,

Well, maybe over their dead bodies isn't a bad idea.

1981

We can bring inflation down and we can get America building again. You know, if that sounds like we're asking for miracles, well, on this eve of St. Patrick's Day, someone with the name of Reagan, I think, is entitled to think in terms of miracles.

You know, there was a lad in court in New York bandaged from his toes to his chin suing for $4 million as a result of an accident and he won the suit. The lawyers for the insurance company went over to him and they said, "You're never going to enjoy a penny of this. We're going to follow you twenty-four hours a day. We know you're faking and the first time you move, we'll have you." He said, "Will you now? Well," he said, "let me tell you what's going to happen to me. They're coming in here with a stretcher. They're taking me out and downstairs, they're putting me in a car—an ambulance. They're driving me straight to Kennedy Airport and they're putting me on the airplane in that stretcher. We're flying direct to Paris, France, and there they're taking me on the stretcher off the plane, putting me in another ambulance. We're going direct to the Shrine of Lourdes and there you're going to see the damndest miracle you ever saw."

March 16, 1981

Remarks of the President at luncheon in Statuary Hall:

I'll speak for my partner, George, for Barbara and Nancy, in responding to this toast. Twice this morning, in the ceremony, was mentioned the fact of the unusualness in this world of what has taken place here today, the orderly transfer, the continuity of government that has gone on, and that I think is the envy of the world.

Now, there's even more of unity represented here today. The crystalware Speaker Tip O'Neill provided from the House side. The plates have come from the Senate. The wine is from California, but I didn't have a thing to do with that.

Washington, D.C.
January 20, 1981

114

Reagan soon realized how much work the presidency en-
tailed. During one of his brief strolls outside the White
House, he said,

This is outside, isn't it?

Washington, D.C.
January 1981

Reagan told his economic advisers,

I come from a warm climate. I enjoy a warm climate.
I'll take a warm climate.

Washington, D.C.
January 1981

At a roast for White House advisor Lyn Nofziger, Reagan
qiopped.

I'm glad the Young Americans for Freedom is having
a fundraiser for Lyn. I hope he can now afford a new suit.

Washington, D.C.

After the successful flight of the space shuttle Columbia,
President Reagan was presented with a gold space flight
jacket by astronauts Young and Crippen. Reagan told them,

You won't mind if I only wear this in the earth's atmosphere?

Reagan attended one evening a dance performance in which
his son, Ron, appeared. After the performance the President
greeted his son, who was still wearing the Swing Era baggy
pants he appeared in during the show:

If I had known you would have needed pants like that,
I would have saved you a bunch of them.

Remarks of the President at the Inaugural Ball:

Hi. Ladies and gentlemen, Nancy and Mike, his wife

Colleen, we're delighted to be here. I know that it can be only for a few minutes because there are ten of these and we're going to get to all of them. And the fellows that are engineering getting us around say it's only going to take four and a half hours.

Washington, D.C.
January 20, 1981

I was taken to task in the press the other day for (saying) *lay*-ison. And they thought that I just didn't know, but I'll tell you, I'm guilty. The army has some words of its own. And when I was a reserve cavalry officer, the army called it *lay*-ison just like they call *oblique* oblike in the army. So now, I'm a civilian so I'll call it liaison.

Washington, D.C.
March 16, 1981

This year we will celebrate a victory won two centuries ago at Yorktown, the victory of a small, fledgling nation over a mighty world power. How many people are aware—I've been told that a British band played the music at that surrender ceremony because we didn't have a band.

Washington, D.C.
March 20, 1981

I also believe that we conservatives, if we mean to continue governing, must realize that it will not always be so easy to place the blame on the past for our national difficulties. You know, one day the great baseball manager Frankie Frisch sent a rookie out to play center field. The rookie promptly dropped the first fly ball that was hit to him. On the next play he let a grounder go between his feet and then threw the ball to the wrong base. Frankie stormed out of the dugout, took his glove away from him, and said,

"I'll show you how to play this position." And the next batter slammed a line drive right over second base. Frankie came in on it, missed it completely, fell down when he tried to chase it, threw down his glove, and yelled at the rookie, "You've got center field so screwed up nobody can play it."

Washington, D.C.
March 20, 1981

Remarks of the President at the dinner of the Conservative Political Action Committee:

Thank you very much. Thank you, Mr. Chairman and Congressman Mickey Edwards, thank you very much. My goodness, I can't realize how much time has gone by because I remember when I first knew Mickey; he was just a clean-shaven boy. But thank you for inviting me here once again. And as Mickey told you, with the exception of those two years, it is true about how often I've been here. So, let me say now that I hope we'll be able to keep this tradition going forward and that you'll invite me again next year. And in the rough days ahead, and I know there will be such days, I hope that you'll be like the mother of the young lad in camp—when the camp director told her that he was going to have to discipline her son. And she said, "Well, don't be too hard on him. He's very sensitive. Slap the boy next to him and that will scare Irving."

Washington, D.C.
March 20, 1981

Remarks of the President at luncheon with Ambassador Sean Donlon:

Thank you very much. Well, I came not bearing gifts of such value, but I did bring a Waterford glass filled with completely green jellybeans.

Mr. Minister, Mr. Ambassador, Mrs. Donlon, honored guests, it goes without saying that I'm delighted to be here on this very special day for the Irish and all who wish they

117

were—and for the lovely music and the young lady who sang so beautifully—your daughter, Mr. Ambassador. You know, it's been said and I've heard all my life that when the Irish sing an Irish song, all who listen wish they were Irish too.

I'm honored to have received your traditional shamrocks which symbolize this day and the friendship between our two countries and I'm especially pleased and most grateful for the beautiful scroll of the Reagan family tree. Up on the Hill this morning at a meeting with some of the legislative leadership—Mr. Speaker, on our side of the aisle—Senator Laxalt presented me with a great green button that he thought I should wear, which said, "Honorary Irishman." And I said to that son of the basques, "I'm not honorary; I am." And now have the proof of it here.

You know, I have to tell you, if you don't mind, a personal note. I am deeply grateful for this because my father was orphaned at age six and I grew up never having heard anything or knowing anything about my family tree, and I would meet other people of the name Reagan or Regan—we're all of the same clan, all cousins, but I tried to say to the secretary one day that his branch of the family just couldn't handle that many letters—then received a letter or a paper from Ireland that told me that in the clan to which we belong, those who said Regan and spelled it that way were the professional people and the educators and only the common laborers called it Reagan. So, meet a common laborer.

But anyway, I am delighted now finally to know what I've never known all my life—the line and the heritage and to where it goes in Ireland. My father also, at the same time, used to tell me and my brother when we were boys—very proudly he would say that in this country the Irish built the jails and then filled them. And I was kind of disturbed at the note of pride in his voice because I'd pictured this in a little different way until I finally learned what he was implying and that was the great high percentage of

the police officers in our land who are Irish.
Remarks of the President at luncheon with Ambassador Sean Donlon

Washington, D.C.
March 17, 1981

The President said a few words to the participants in Ford's Theater Gala before the curtain rose:

It's our pleasure to host you all here tonight. And I know that we all look forward to the performance that's going to follow at Ford's Theater. You know, one of the great benefits we found of living here is you get to be a part of the great history of this beautiful city. Now, I used the word "benefit" there. For some who are among us tonight—you realize that word has a very singular meaning. A benefit in the entertainment world is any occasion where the actors are performing without pay. And I learned at first on such occasions, if you don't sing or dance, you usually wind up introducing someone who does.

I remember one such occasion when there were seven of us lined up to introduce Nelson Eddy singing "Shortenin' Bread." If you did that enough, that usually led to your being an after-dinner speaker. And as that went on, you could talk your way right out of show business into another line of work.

After the performance, Ronald Reagan had a few concluding thoughts:

Nancy and I have been very honored to be a part of this and I think that I speak for everyone here when I say a heartfelt thanks to these fine artists who have given their time and their talent to make this evening so wonderful.

You know, some people were mentioned, some credits given—you couldn't name all of the people here in this theater that have had a hand in making this very wonderful evening. One was mentioned, Frankie Hewitt, and she certainly deserves it. There were two ladies that I don't think anybody will mind if I mention who worked long and tirelessly together to make this a success: Mrs. Tip O'Neill and Mrs. Howard Baker.

They worked so well together that I've got a couple of projects I'm going to suggest to their husbands. It is worth a try. This place is so much a part of our heritage, reminds us so much of our traditions—and incidentally, it is not true I used to play this theater before it closed.

Washington, D.C.
March 21, 1981

Reagan's top aide told him, "We don't ever want to see a picture of you kissing [Soviet leader] Brezhnev," referring to the ceremony in which President Carter kissed the Soviet leader. Reagan replied,

You won't even see me kissing Brezhnev's wife!

Washington, D.C.
1981

While visiting the Canadian Parliament, Reagan, after thanking the Canadians for such exports as Art Linkletter and Mary Pickford, remarked that the demonstrators who protested his visit

must have been imported to make me feel at home.

1981

Remarks of the President at the Salute to Congress Dinner:
Thank you very much and thank you especially for not giving me a question.

I'm a little surprised to find myself at this podium tonight. I know your organization was founded by six Washington newspaperwomen in 1919. It seems only yesterday.

120

I know that it was Washington's National Press Club for over half a century, so I thought that tonight's production would be equal time, right? A night for Nancy. Then I learned of your 1971 pioneering and coeducational Washington press corps. You changed the name. You admitted male members. You also encouraged male speakers. So here I am, a poor but modest substitute for the former Nancy Davis, ready to defend myself and every other middle-aged male in America.

Washington, D.C.
February 4, 1981

On his busy schedule:

I have no time to be President.

1981

When asked whether a certain program couldn't be reduced even further, Reagan told a cabinet secretary:

Go ahead and cut it. They're going to hang me in effigy anyway, and it doesn't matter how high.

1981

God bless all of you. And thank you for what you're doing because in those cities, the proceeds are going to the local charities of those communities where the balls are being held. You look very pretty tonight (addressing Mrs. Reagan). I think she looks gorgeous as a matter of fact. On the way over someone said when we got here, we might even have a minute or two to dance, but I don't think so. Well, they've got us in public housing and we'll dance when we get the heck there.

At the Inaugural Ball
Washington, D.C.
January 20, 1981

121

Mike Deaver, assistant to the President, is believed by many to be closest to Reagan. The press has often remarked on their "father and son" relationship. Aware of the press's view, Reagan said to Deaver at a White House concert:

You can come over here, son, and sit by me.

Washington, D.C.
1981

Differences among his aides moved Reagan to observe,

Sometimes our right hand doesn't know what our far right hand is doing.

Washington, D.C.
1981

Remarks of the president at roast in honor of Jim Brady:

Well, I just have to tell you that, Jim, we've been looking all over for you. Headline news breaking all around us, I've declared martial law, dismissed the Congress. And here I find you fraternizing.

I understand that this is something in the nature of, well, shall we say a roast, and I don't know whether Jim is prepared for that yet or not. Here you are. And, therefore, I would like to ask all of you—you know, there's still a long way to go on our honeymoon and Nancy says he's "Y and H." So, even though—that means young and handsome. So please be gentle. And, Jim, you're not to take seriously anything they say.

MR. BRADY: I never do.

As a matter of fact, don't take anything seriously that I've said so far. But I will be serious for a minute. I think that this is borne out of respect and affection that are widespread among these people and that you have earned. And let's cancel the lottery. Or were you going to promise that later?

MR. BRADY: I didn't want to make any unilateral conces-
sions, and now you've given it away.

Well, that's one of the major decisions we've made.
We've got some minor things going on like El Salvador,
Afghanistan, and so forth. But you can see that when it
comes to the big decisions, we make them fast.

Well, anyway, I'm glad that we could drop by here and
I'm glad that you're all doing this and I'm very glad that
Jim is where he is, and I mean that seriously, in our admin-
istration.

Enjoy it. We're on our way to Ford's Theater.
Washington, D.C.
March 21, 1981

*When asked whether the President had denied a federal
appointment to a woman who publicly disagreed with his
budget cuts, Reagan turned the question around on himself.*

How can you say that about a sweet fellow like me?
Washington, D.C.
March 30, 1981

*After his opening remarks at his second press conference,
Reagan said,*

And now we shall get on with our first attempt at
"Reagan roulette."

Speaking to reporters by phone, the President said,

Well, I'm up at Camp David. We're getting a little used
to it now, but I have to tell you the first time I came to this
place, to Camp David, Ed Meese sewed nametags in all my
undershorts and T-shirts.
Camp David, Md.
April 25, 1981

123

On the budget and Congress:

Cures were developed for which there were no known diseases.

1981

The rule says, if it ain't broke, don't fix it.

1981

Going through the lists of budget cuts, the President was asked, "Can you stand the political heat on his one?" Replied Reagan,

Look, I come from a warm climate . . . I can stand the heat.

Washington, D.C.
January 1981

Remarks of the President at luncheon for Baseball Hall of Fame members:

The nostalgia is bubbling within me, and I may have to be dragged out of here because of all the stories that are coming up in my mind. Baseball—I had finally to confess over here, no, I didn't play when I was young. I went down the football path. I did play in a way, as Bob Lemon well knows, I was old Alex—Grover Cleveland Alexander, and I've been very proud of that. It was a wonderful experience. There were quite a few ballplayers, including Bob Lemon, who were on the set for that picture. And I remember one day when they wanted some shots of me pitching, but kind of close up—so they wanted me to throw past the camera and they had a fellow back there—Al Lyons, one of the ballplayers—that was going to catch the ball and then toss it back over the camera to me, and the camera was getting these close shots for use wherever they could. And he was on one side of the camera and my control wasn't all that it should be at one point and I threw it on the other side of the camera. And he speared it with his left hand with no glove on. He was a lefthander, and after he brought the ball

124

to me, he said, "Alex, I'm sorry I had to catch your blazer barehanded."

He didn't suffer any pain, I am sure. But I remember we had a fellow that I'm sure some of you know and remember, Metrovich. And Metrovich, during the day's shooting, would memorize everyone's lines. And then if we were on location and would get into the bus to go back in from location, he would play all the scenes for us on the bus. So, thinking about this one day on the process screen, an umpire behind him—he was at the plate, and they wanted a shot of a ballplayer at the plate—and the director said, "There are no lines but you'll know what to say." He said, "The umpire's going to call it a strike," and he said, "You don't think it's a strike. So do what you do in a ball game when you think it's a bad call." And extroverted Metrovich, who was happy to play all the scenes, was standing up at the plate and if you looked closely, you could see that the bat was beginning to shake a little bit—and the ball came by on an afterplay and the umpire bellows—bellowed out—"Strike one." And Metrovich lowered the bat and he says, "Gee, that was no strike." The picture wasn't a comedy so we couldn't leave it in. But you know, I've always been sorry about one thing. Alex is in the Hall of Fame and deservedly so. Everyone knows that great 1926 World Series. He had won two games, and then was called on in the seventh inning with the bases loaded, no one out, and one of the most dangerous hitters in baseball at the plate. And he came in and saved the game.

The tragedy that I've always regretted is that the studio was unwilling to reveal in the picture, was afraid to reveal what I think was the best kept secret in sports. A bad habit of Alex's was widely heralded and took something away from his luster. But they wouldn't let us use the actual word of what was behind, maybe, his bad habit. Alex was an epileptic. And when he was arrested and picked up for being drunk in a gutter, as he once was, he wasn't drunk at all. But he would rather take that than admit to the disease that plagued him all his life. But he also, early in his baseball career, was hit in the head going from first base down to second, on a throw from second; they caught him right in the head and he was out of baseball for a while and they didn't know whether forever because he had double vision. And he kept experimenting, trying to find out if there wasn't some way that he could pitch. And he went to a minor league club and asked for a tryout and the manager got up at the plate and said, "Well, go out on the mound and throw me a few." Alex broke three of his ribs on the first pitch. His experiment had been to close one eye—and the friend that was with him when they were thrown out of the ballpark said, "What happened?" And he said, "I closed the wrong eye."

But there are men in this room that were playing when I was broadcasting and I promised to say something here to a great Cub fan that we have at the table that would make him feel good. I was broadcasting the Cubs when the only mathematical possibility, and Billy Herman will remember this very well, that the Cubs had of winning the pennant was to win the last twenty-one games of the season. And they did. And I was so imbued with baseball by that time that I knew you're not supposed to talk about a no-hitter while it's going on because you'll jinx him. So there I was, a broadcaster, and never mentioned once in the twenty-one games, and I was getting as uptight as they were, and never mentioned the fact that they were at sixteen, they were at seventeen, and that they hadn't lost a game because I was afraid I'd jinx them. But anyway, they did it and it's still in the record books. What isn't in the record books is Billy Jurges staying at the plate I think the longest of any ballplayer in the history of the game. I was doing the games by telegraphic report and the fellow on the other side of a window with a little slit underneath, the headphones on, getting the dot and dash Morse code from the ballpark would type out the play and paper would come through to me—it would say, "SlC." Well, you're not going to sell any Wheaties yelling SlC. So I'd say, "And so-and-so comes out of the wind-up, here's the pitch. And it's a called strike

126

breaking over the outside corner to so-and-so, who'd rather have a ball some place else and so forth and banged out there.''

Well, I saw him start to type and I started—Dizzy Dean was on the mound and I started the ball on the way to the plate. In the wind-up Curly, the fellow on the other side, was shaking his head and I thought just maybe it was a miraculous play or something, but when the slip came through it said, ''The wire's gone dead.'' Well, I had the ball on the way to the plate. And I figured real quick, I could say we'll tell them what had happened and then play transcribed music, but in those days there were at least seven or eight other fellows that were doing the same ball game. I didn't want to lose the audience. So I thought real quick, ''There's one thing that doesn't get in the score book,'' so I had Billy foul one off. And I looked at Curly and Curly just went like this, so I had him foul another one. And I had him foul one back of third base and described the fight between the two kids that were trying to get the ball. Then I had him foul one that just missed being a home run, by about a foot and a half. And I did set a world record for successive fouls or for someone standing there except that no one keeps records of that kind and I was beginning to sweat when Curly sat up straight and started typing, he was nodding his head, ''Yes.'' And the slip came through the window and I could hardly talk for laughing because it said, ''Jurges popped out on the first ball pitched.''

But those were wonderful days, not only playing the part, but some of you here, I think, will—I'm going to tell another story here that has been confirmed for me by Waite Hoyt. Those of you who played when the Dodgers were in Brooklyn, know that Brooklynites have a tendency to refer to someone by the name of Earl as ''Oil.'' But if they want a quart of oil in the car, they say, ''Give me a quart of earl.'' And Waite was sliding into second and he twisted his ankle and instead of getting up he was lying there, and there was a deep hush over the whole ballpark and then a

127

Brooklyn voice was heard above all that silence, ''Gee, hurt is Hoyt.''

Washington, D.C.
March 27, 1981